WOMEN'S POLITICAL PARTICIPATION AND GOOD GOVERNANCE: 21ST CENTURY CHALLENGES

**UNITED NATIONS
DEVELOPMENT PROGRAMME**

**UNITED NATIONS
DEVELOPMENT PROGRAMME**

DBN: 1660995

The United Nations Development Programme is the UN's
largest source of grant for development co-operation. Its funding
is from voluntary contributions of Member States of the United
Nations and affiliated agencies. A network of 132 country offices—
and programmes in more than 170 countries and territories—helps
people to help themselves. In each of these countries, the UNDP
Resident Representative normally also serves as the Resident
Coordinator of operational activities for development of the
United Nations system as a whole. This can include humanitarian
as well as development assistance.

UNDP's main priority is poverty eradication. Its work also focuses on
the closely linked goals of environmental regeneration, the creation
of sustainable livelihoods and the empowerment of women. Programmes
for good governance and peace-building create a climate for progress
in these areas. Country and regional programmes draw on the
expertise of developing country nationals and non-governmental
organisations, the specialised agencies of the UN system and
research institutes. Seventy-five per cent of all UNDP-supported
projects are implemented by local organisations.

Ninety per cent of UNDP's core programme is focused on 66
countries that are home to 90 per cent of the world's extremely
poor. UNDP is a hands-on organisation with 85 per cent of its
staff in the countries that it supports.

Information on UNDP's governance-related policies could be found
on the web site: http://magnet.undp.org/

UN2
DP
2000W56

TABLE OF CONTENTS

WOMEN'S
POLITICAL
PARTICIPATION
AND GOOD
GOVERNANCE:
21ST CENTURY
CHALLENGES

FOREWORD

Gender equality and the empowerment of women are critical dimensions of the United Nations Development Programme's efforts to help meet the overarching goal of halving world poverty by 2015. The launch of this publication during the General Assembly Special Session on Beijing +5 testifies to UNDP's commitment to keeping these issues among its top priorities. The studies it contains clearly show how, despite substantial obstacles, women decision makers in developing countries have already begun to put a distinctive stamp on governance mechanisms, institutions and broader political debates. But it also draws attention to the fact that much more still needs to be done.

This publication draws on the experiences and expertise of ministers, members of parliament, government officials and members of national, grassroots civil society and the private sector, who participated in a UNDP-sponsored meeting on Women's Political Participation—21st Century Challenges (New Delhi, March 1999). It focuses on a number of issues including progress made in women's political participation since Beijing, the Indian experiment with constitutional amendments mandating the reservation of one third of local government-elected representation to women, and the wider connection between gender, poverty and governance. It also highlights the South African Women's Budget, Uganda's experience with new political alliances for gender and politics and explores the policy responses to gender-based violence.

One central theme is that the continued absence of women's voices in governance is largely due to inequitable representation and participation in institutional structures, from governments and political parties to NGOs and the private sector. However, it also recognizes that boosting women's political participation needs to go beyond raw numbers to encompass the complex relationship between power, poverty and participation. Women want and need to be able to participate in the decisions that affect them, their families, communities and countries.

There are several ways to help achieve these goals. These include establishing new mechanisms that allow women directly to influence broader political and economic measures, particularly the allocations of national budgets. It also means taking advantage of the unprecedented opportunities for national, regional and global networking and alliance-building made possible by recent advances in information technology, particularly the internet. UNDP is committed to working with governments, civil society and other partners to use these and other initiatives to advance more inclusive and effective forms of governance at all levels of society.

Mark Malloch Brown
Administrator
United Nations Development Programme

WOMEN'S
POLITICAL
PARTICIPATION
AND GOOD
GOVERNANCE:
**21ST CENTURY
CHALLENGES**

PREFACE

Since the early 1990s, UNDP has progressively implemented the sustainable human development approach in its efforts to promote development that not only generates economic growth, but also distributes its benefits equitably, regenerates the environment rather than destroying it and empowers men and women rather than marginalising them. This type of development depends on good governance, including the empowerment of individuals and communities.

The UNDP Global Programme for Governance, launched in 1997, focused on six areas: institutions of governance, public and private sector management and accountability, decentralisation and local governance, civil society organisations and governance in special circumstances. Gender issues cut across all these areas. In New York in July 1997, UNDP held its International Conference on Governance and Sustainable Growth and Equity, a global meeting organised in four forums: the Ministerial/Senior Officials Forum, the Mayors Colloquium, the Parliamentarians' Forum and the Civil Society Organisations Dialogue. Governance actors in all four of these domains mingled before and after the formal meetings of their respective groups over three days and gathered together in a final session to hear the report of each forum.

In this broad context, the Conference highlighted a close relationship between the low number of women parliamentarians and the high number of women in poverty. It also underscored that the budget of any nation is the most important economic instrument for improving the well-being of its citizens. This reconfirmed what gender specialists have always maintained: that unless macroeconomic policies are engendered and adequate budgetary allocations for health, education and social support systems are earmarked, an increasing number of women and their families will continue their drift into poverty. The Conference also called upon countries that have attained a 30 per cent representation of women in their parliaments to share their experience and strategies with others.

UNDP defines governance as the exercise of economic, political and administrative authority to manage a country's affairs at all levels. It comprises the mechanisms, processes and institutions through which citizens and groups articulate their interests, exercise their legal rights, meet their obligations and mediate their differences. The marginalisation of women in the political process and governance in general has been both the cause and effect of the slow progress made in the advancement of women. For this reason, the Management Development and Governance Division of the Bureau for Development Policy in United Nations Development convened a meeting on Women's Political Participation: 21st Century Challenges, held in New Delhi between 24 and 26 March 1999. It engaged women politicians and representatives of civil society from all regions, covered by UNDP, in a dialogue

WOMEN'S
POLITICAL
PARTICIPATION
AND GOOD
GOVERNANCE:
21ST CENTURY
CHALLENGES

to promote the sharing of experience and to build alliances.

The present report documents this exchange and presents a variety of conclusions in the hope that this particular undertaking in collective learning will help accelerate progress for women, men and children of both genders and that it will contribute significantly to the forthcoming stock-taking and recommendations of Beijing+5—Special Session of the General Assembly, Women 2000: Gender Equality, Development and Peace for the Twenty-first Century, 5-9 June 2000.

G. Shabbir Cheema
Director
Management Development and Governance Division
Bureau for Development Policy
United Nations Development Programme

WOMEN'S
POLITICAL
PARTICIPATION
AND GOOD
GOVERNANCE:
21ST CENTURY
CHALLENGES

iv

ACKNOWLEDGEMENTS

ACKNOWLEDGEMENTS

The Management Development and Governance Division of the Bureau for Development Policy appreciates the support and commitment that the United Nations Development Programme Office in New Delhi has provided to making possible the meeting on Women's Political Participation: Challenges for the 21st Century. It is particularly grateful for the support provided by Ms. Brenda Gayle McSweeney, United Nations Resident Coordinator and Representative of United Nations Development Programme (UNDP), New Delhi, India; Richard Conroy, Deputy Resident Representative; and Mr. R. Sudarshan, Chief of the Governance Division. Particular thanks go to Ms. Kalyani Menon-Sen, for having been the right arm for this meeting.

Our special thanks also go to Mrs. Usha Narayanan, First Lady of India, for agreeing to give the keynote speech at the meeting and providing her personal support; to Dr. Najma Haptulla, Deputy Chairperson of Rajya Sabha, India, and UNDP Distinguished Human Development Ambassador, who is currently President of the Inter-Parliamentary Union; and to Ms. Vibha Parathasarthy, Chairperson of the National Commission for Women of India, who not only addressed the meeting, but provided valuable insights. Others who made significant contributions were Sally Baden, Debbie Budlender, Azza Karram, Poornima Vyasalu, Paul Oquist and Sajjad Naseer.

The present collection is the product of all the participants in the New Delhi meeting (listed in Annex 1). The volume was conceived and managed by Lina Hamadeh-Banerjee, Senior Programme Advisor for Gender and Governance of the UNDP Management and Governance Development Division, who also organised the meeting. Shawna Tropp furnished editorial skill in shaping and refining the manuscript.

WOMEN'S
POLITICAL
PARTICIPATION
AND GOOD
GOVERNANCE:
21ST CENTURY
CHALLENGES

OVERVIEW: WOMEN'S POLITICAL PARTICIPATION AND GOOD GOVERNANCE: 21ST CENTURY CHALLENGES

LINA HAMADEH-BANERJEE AND PAUL OQUIST[1]

Ironies of Democracy

The movement for gender equality of late 20th century is closely linked to the human rights movement. But the concept of *women's participation in governance on an equal footing with men* dates back at least to the 4th century BCE. The Greek philosopher Plato put it into the mouth of his mentor, Socrates, in *The Republic* as "part of the natural relation of the sexes". The notion did not strike Socrates' young listeners in ancient Athens as altogether radical. They saw women—though largely a privileged few—openly active in the political system. Aspasia, the mistress of the 5th century leader Pericles, had wielded considerable political power visibly. In the rival city-state of Sparta, the mothers of potential warriors had significant political rights. Plato was no democrat, but his experience had led him to conclude that intelligence and ethics were not limited to any one class, ethnicity or gender. He believed passionately that education could cultivate these qualities in individuals—and that those who benefited most from education could and should govern others. His ideal polity was a benevolent meritocracy.[2]

If we hurtle into modern times, we find that two years before the French Revolution of 1789, Condorcet, author of the *Progress of the Human Mind*, proposed that women be declared eligible for election to governing bodies.[3] Again, the idea was not a terribly radical departure from a number of practices throughout Western Europe. Women of property had often voted in local councils; many women over many centuries had wielded power behind the throne; a good number had ruled whole nations, whether as regents or in their own right. France now stood—albeit very briefly—on the edge of democracy.

Condorcet was a nobleman, a marquis as well as a mathematician, philosopher and passionate advocate for universal education. But a self-educated butcher's

---

[1] Lina Hamadeh-Banerjee is Senior Programme Advisor on Gender and Governance in UNDP. Paul Oquist is Chief of the Governance Unit in the UNDP Country Office in Islamabad, Pakistan.

[2] Plato, *The Republic*, translated by Benjamin Jowett. Our thanks to Shawna Tropp for this reminder, as well as for others from Western intellectual history.

[3] For a bird's-eye view of these developments, see Mim Kelber, editor, *Women and Government: New Ways to Political Power*, Westport and London, Praeger, 1994, pp. 1- 61. Condorcet was also a passionate believer in universal education and strongly opposed slavery.

daughter, Olympe de Gouges, led women of all classes in presenting a women's reform agenda to the National Assembly in October 1789. Shortly thereafter, she proclaimed that the new French Declaration on the Rights of Man negated the principle of natural equality because it excluded people from citizenship on the basis of gender and race. Even before her middle-class English contemporary, Mary Wollstonecraft, had published her *Vindication of the Rights of Women* in 1792, Gouges had written and issued a Declaration on the Rights of Women. She continued to organise her female compatriots in packing the galleries of successive French legislative bodies during the Revolution. In 1793, as the ostensibly democratic Committee on Public Security unleashed what came to be known as the "Reign of Terror", it beheaded Gouges and outlawed women's political associations.[4]

With parallel developments earlier in the new United States of America and later in Great Britain, the rebirth of democracy in the modern West went hand in hand with the disenfranchisement of women. For more than a century after the French Revolution, western women went on losing the few political rights that their privileged sisters had held before. Only in 1893 did any western democracy—New Zealand—grant women the right to vote.

Although the world-wide movement for women's equality took new impetus from the birth of the United Nations and the promulgation of the 1948 Universal Declaration of Human Rights, it was not until the preparations for the First World Conference on Women, which took place in Mexico City in 1975, that the international community took systematic stock of the inequities that continued to render women second-class citizens in every country, including the industrialised democracies of the western world. In 1979, for the first time in history, women's rights took codified form in an international human rights instrument. The Convention on the Elimination of All Forms of Discrimination Against Women (CEDAW) has been in force only since 1981. Currently, 139 countries—more than two thirds of the Member States of the United Nations—are parties to the treaty. Another 44 have acceded to the treaty with reservations on certain provisions of the text. Women's participation in governance, however, still lags far behind that of men.

The Present Report and its Background

This report shows that until gender parity is reached in governance, women cannot reach full equality with men in any sphere. The absence of women's voices in shaping the most fundamental political instruments—the most critical of which is the national budget—has ensured the preservation of gender inequity even with regard to women's health and security in their own homes.

It is therefore no accident that the UNDP Management Development and Governance Division convened a meeting on Women's Political Participation: 21st Century Challenges. Held in New Delhi, India from 24–26 March 1999, it brought together women parliamentarians, planners and civil society representatives, including those of grassroots organisations, to take stock of women's presence in government structures and to make recommendations for overcoming the fundamental obstacle that women face in politics: the enduring division of the "public" and "private" spheres that relegates women to the latter.

The New Delhi meeting built on a number of others, notably the February 1997 conference of the International Parliamentary Union entitled "Towards Partnership between Men and Women in Politics". A few months later, UNDP's International Conference on Governance for Sustainable Growth and Equity, held in New York in July 1997, drew attention, *inter alia*, to the low number of women parliamentarians and the high number of women in poverty. Subsequently, the Conference on Good Governance and Gender sponsored by the Netherlands Ministry of Foreign Affairs and held in Harare, Zimbabwe from 18–20 May 1998, was largely devoted to inequities in the enabling environment for women—among these education, training, ownership of the means of production or even decision-making power in the home that might be translated into the public sphere.

The *UNDP Human Development Report 1995* showed that in no society do women enjoy the same opportunities as men. It also demonstrated that successful initiatives for removing gender inequalities do not depend on wealth of nations. And even though some countries have set targets for women's representation in national government

---

[4] Condorcet was also arrested on the recommendation of the Committee and killed himself in his prison cell.

structures, these often do not have significant impact elsewhere in governance. Nor have these targets, even when achieved, endured. Moreover, statistical data and analysis on decision-making in the private sector and in local government is incomplete. Finally, as most of the current statistics come from developed countries, the strategies recommended for increasing women's political participation are often focused on models from these polities that do not meet the needs of developing nations.

Earlier research carried out by the UN Research Institute on Social Development (UNRISD) with funding from UNDP is summed up in *Technical Co-operation and Women's Lives: Integrating Gender into Development Policy.*[5] It reviewed the experiences of development institutions in addressing development policies and programmes in seven countries and highlighted the need to engender macroeconomic policies and to bring together different national actors that influence these policies. It also recognised that the men elected to the executive and legislative branches of government, who hold the key to decision-making for development priorities, planning and expenditure, are largely unaware of household needs and the ways in which these relate to socio-economic development at the community, local, provincial and national levels.

Taking Stock

Considerable progress has taken place in women's political participation, particularly towards the end of this century. Despite this progress, however, the 21st century begins with enormous unfinished business in this realm.

Achievements

Twenty five years after the First World Conference on Women in Mexico City, more than 20 after CEDAW, and five after the Fourth World Conference in Beijing, gender equality has finally been inscribed on the political agenda of most of the world. For example, the Beijing Platform for Action set the goal of 30 per cent for women in national decision-making positions, as a milestone toward the ultimate objective of 50 per cent. Five years after Beijing, the level of women in parliaments in the world has

increased from 10 per cent to 12 per cent. However, regional variations are significant. They range from 37.6 per cent in the Nordic countries to 15.5 per cent in the Americas, 13.4 per cent in Asia, 12.5 per cent in Europe excluding the Nordic countries, 11.6 per cent in Sub-Saharan Africa, 8.3 per cent in the Pacific and 3.3 per cent in the Arab states. Since Beijing, women speakers of parliament have been named for the first time in six countries: Ethiopia (1995), Latvia (1995), Peru (1995), Jamaica (1996), Malta (1996) and Poland (1997).

With regard to ministerial and sub-ministerial positions, two countries have reached over 30 per cent representation for women (Sweden and the Bahamas). At the other end of the spectrum, there are 15 countries in which there is no presence of women in these posts (Afghanistan, Bahrain, Djibouti, Lebanon, Monaco, Myanmar, Nauru, Nepal, Saudi Arabia, the Solomon Islands, Somalia, United Arab Emirates and Yemen). Six women are currently presidents or prime ministers: Bangladesh (Prime Minister), Guyana (President), Ireland (President), New Zealand (Prime Minister) and Sri Lanka (President and Prime Minister),

At the local level, the International Association of Local Authorities (IULA) has set the goal of not more than 60 per cent of either gender represented in local assemblies. It also points out that information on the current situation in local assemblies is incomplete. Estimates on woman as local counselors are 23 per cent in the United States, 20 per cent for Europe (ranging from 40 per cent in Sweden to 4 per cent in Greece), 18 per cent in Canada, less than 5 per cent in Africa and 3.8 per cent in Latin America. No estimate is available for Asia.

Differences by sector are significant in all countries. For example, Sweden has the highest percentage of women in parliament (44 per cent), but less than 10 per cent of women in senior academic positions, while in Egypt women constitute less than 2 per cent of Parliament, but over 40 per cent of senior academic staff.

The Road Ahead

Women want to influence the decisions that affect their lives and the lives of their families, the political economy and destiny of their communities and nations, as well as the structure of international relations. Political participation and representation is essential for the achievement of these ends. This will allow women and men of all ages and races the full exercise of their human rights. It is also the avenue for influencing equitable resource allocations for development that shape the lives of girls and boys, as well as women and men.

There is growing recognition that economic participation and political participation cannot be separated. Institutional transformations are needed to create the enabling environment for the economic and political empowerment of women. A more profound understanding of the barriers in labour markets and remuneration processes is also necessary as a precondition for their transformation. This is particularly important since women's economic independence is critical for their exercise of influence on decisions that affect their lives and their families.

There are strong linkages between processes that lead to poverty and those that result in gender disparities. Efforts at poverty reduction therefore need to be informed by a gender analysis. Transforming and increasing the accountability of institutions to women's interests, and especially the interests of poor women, is necessary for poverty reduction and good governance.

The feminization of poverty manifests itself differently in different contexts. In many contexts, the poor in general and other disadvantaged groups share many of the conditions and needs represented by the women's movement for equity, inclusion, participation and representation. In many instances at present, they also suffer disproportionately from the impact of globalisation on their livelihoods. For example, with liberalisation of the economy in India, multinational corporations have entered into the production of goods earlier made by the poor, women in particular, and have pushed poor women out of their traditional livelihood niches.

Greater levels of transparency and accountability, including rapid responsiveness to citizen demands, are necessary to strengthen good governance. They also constitute the conditions necessary for advances in gender equity. Uganda, for instance, has experimented with transparency measures for making government disbursement information available to the public: with a push from its Women's Caucus, the Ugandan Parliament made it mandatory that funds allocated for communities must be made public. Indeed, as a recent World Bank study indicates, a decrease in corruption in government may be linked to an increase in women's political participation.[6]

Politics and participation range from the home through the locality to the national level. Women need to participate at the micro level of the home, the meso level of community organisations and local government, and at the macro level of national party, parliamentary and governmental politics. Decentralisation, with its devolution of power and resources, appears to be opening more scenarios for the meaningful participation and representation of women.

The Scope of this Report

In preparation for this meeting, UNDP commissioned four background papers, all of them included as chapters in this publication. Additional chapters place these commissioned studies within a wider perspective and also supplement them with additional analysis and a review of discussions during the New Delhi meeting. The Management and Governance Development Division has also divided the entire work into three parts, respectively entitled "Concepts", "Cases" and "Conclusions".

After this initial Overview, the first of the "Concepts" chapters, *Women's Agency in Governance*, sets out the framework for viewing the papers commissioned for the meeting. It analyses the impact of women as agents of change in the political process, reviews key challenges in this area and suggests strategies for increasing women's representation.

Chapter 3, *Beijing + 5: Women's Political Participation: Review of Strategies, Trends and Future Projections* examines progress made since the Beijing Conference in relation to women's representation in parliaments, premiership and local government. Its primary message is the need to go beyond numbers in women's political representation and to demonstrate the impact of women's participation at the decision-making level

WOMEN'S POLITICAL PARTICIPATION AND GOOD GOVERNANCE: 21ST CENTURY CHALLENGES

⁶ David Dollar, Raymond Fisman and Roberta Gatti, *Are Women Really the 'Fairer' Sex,: Corruption and Women in Government*, Policy Research Report on Gender and Development, Working Paper Series, No. 4, Development Economics Research Group, Washington, DC, 1999.

in politics. Its recommendations cover, among other subjects: filling the vacuum of information, statistics, analysis and comparison regarding women's political participation, the development of indicators on the impact of women's political representation on engendering the political agenda and remunerative rewards to governments for achievements in gender-sensitive governance.

Chapter 4, *Gender, Governance and the Feminization of Poverty*, argues that poverty is an economic and a political issue that works against both women and the poor in general. It examines the relationship between poverty and women and points out the following: (a) women have a higher *incidence* of poverty than men; (b) women's poverty is more severe than that of men; and (c) there is a trend to greater poverty among women, particularly associated with the rising rates of female-headed households. The chapter also questions the validity of using the income of households as the basis for analysis in developing poverty reduction strategies. Finally, it examines governance structures and processes to promote poverty reduction in general and to respond specifically to women's experience of poverty.

Chapter 5, *Women in the Panchayti Raj: Grassroots Democracy in India* is the first case study of this report. It focuses on the Indian experience with local government as a result of the constitutional amendments that reserved one third of the seats in local assemblies, the Panchayati raj, to women and thereby sweeping almost one million women into elective politics throughout the country. The chapter shows that the experience so far has showed mixed results in addressing social injustice and other issues of poverty. It concludes, however, that grassroots leadership is a testing-ground for women's political participation at the national level and that community development work often serves as training ground for women entering local politics.

Chapter 6, *The South African Women's Budget Initiative*, documents this well-known initiative, the result of an alliance between women parliamentarians, women in the civil service and civil society, that served as a "shadow" engendered national budget. The budget analysis is based on the premise that budget follows policy—not vice-versa— and therefore approaches budget allocations through analysis of (a) gender-

specific expenditure, (b) expenditures that promote gender equity within public service, such as affirmative action, and (c) mainstream expenditure. It then suggests a range of alternatives.

Chapter 7, *Alliances for Gender and Politics: The Ugandan Women's Caucus* documents the Ugandan experience as a case study. This experience highlights the ways in which women have succeeded in impacting political and socio-economic development in one country that has undergone more than two decades of upheaval and impoverishment.

Chapter 8, *Crossing the Governance Private Threshold: the Experience of the Gender Violence Campaign in Latin America and the Caribbean*, presents the experience of the United Nations Inter-agency Campaign against Gender Violence in Latin America and the Caribbean. The last case study of this report, it indicates the pitfalls of shielding violence in the home by distinctions of where crimes take place.

Finally, the report contains three chapters of conclusion. Chapter 9, *A Voice of Their Own: Conclusions of the New Delhi Meeting on Women's Political Participation*, sums up the recommendations made by participants in this meeting.

Chapters 10 and 11 are devoted to the two issues the participants considered critical. Chapter 10, entitled *Think Globally, Elect Locally?* looks world-wide at the implications of women's participation in local government structures. Chapter 11, *Budgets: the Political Bottom Line*, concentrates on engendering the governance instrument that ultimately determines the nature of any country's socio-economic development.

Finally, the collection's annexes contain a note of appreciation to the participants in the meeting, the Recommendations of the Beijing Platform for Action relevant to decision-making and UNDP's experience in the realm of gender and governing institutions.

BIBLIOGRAPHY

Dollar, D., R. Fisman and R. Gatti (1999). *Are Women Really the 'Fairer' Sex: Corruption and Women in Government*, Policy Research Report on Gender and Development, Working Paper Series, No. 4, Development Economics Research Group, Washington, DC.

Kelber, M., ed., (1994). *Women and Government: New Ways to Political Power*, Westport and London, Praeger.

Sen, A. (1990). "More than 100 Million Women are Missing", the *New York Review of Books* 37:20, December 20 issue.

UNDP (1995). *Human Development Report 1995*, UNDP, New York.

PART I : CONCEPTS

WOMEN'S AGENCY IN GOVERNANCE

LINA HAMADEH-BANERJEE

Welfare and Agency

In *Development as Freedom*, the Nobel Laureate Amartya Sen[7] recalls Mary Wollenstonecraft's 1792 classic *Vindication of the Rights of Woman* to illustrate the distinction between women as beneficiaries of the development process whose well-being it enhances—the "welfare" approach to enhancing women's status—and women as agents of development, as movers and shapers of change that benefits men and children as well—the "agency" approach. Sen looks back even further than the revolution Wollstonecraft was advocating as an exile in Paris while the French Revolution swirled about her, excluding women from the political changes sweeping Europe at that time. He recalls the medieval idea of agent and patient:

> "... the role of a person as an 'agent' is fundamentally distinct from (though not independent of) the role of the same person as a 'patient'. The fact that the agent may have to see herself as a patient as well does not alter the additional modalities and responsibilities that are inescapably associated with the agency of a person. ... not only are we well or ill, but we also act or refuse to act, and can choose to act one way rather than another. And thus we—women and men—must take responsibility for doing things or not doing them. It makes a difference...."

In most countries, the "less-than-equal" status of women to men still prevails, prompting a welfarist approach to the advancement of women—even in efforts to "mainstream" gender issues by governments, civil society, bilateral and multilateral development agencies. This tendency belies and even denies the idea that women are responsible persons, not only capable of making choices, but necessary to this process in any democratic society.

This concept is the perspective within which we must appraise every effort to meet the 21st century challenges to women's political participation.

As Sen, among others, points out, such factors as literacy, education, earning power, an economic role outside the family and access to property rights have contributed to women's assuming independent voice and agency, particularly in

WOMEN'S POLITICAL PARTICIPATION AND GOOD GOVERNANCE: 21ST CENTURY CHALLENGES

---

[7] Amartya Sen, *Development as Freedom*, Alfred A. Knopf, New York, 1999.

the family. The enormous literature on women's education and employment in their empowerment and emancipation is still growing. Numerous studies have also demonstrated the improvement of nutritional intake in the household as a result of women's independent income. Research in India has shown a correlation between women's education and economic independence and increased child survival rates[8] and, as UNFPA analysis over the years has illustrated, increasing educational attainment among women correlates closely with lower fertility rates and their impact on population growth.

Women's participation in politics cannot be isolated from their overall socio-economic status, the following factors in particular: Women usually do not have equal access with men to the means for participation, such as the enabling skills acquired through education and training or controlling the means of production or access to the information media, including the new communications technologies. They often do not have decision-making power within the household to translate into the public sphere; in many developing countries, their possessions, including land and other collateral, are legally the property of their husbands, fathers or sons.[9] For this very reason, they have not been able to overcome gender biases and other barriers that obstruct their access to political decision-making. Further, because of increasing trends in most countries, including the industrialised nations, to the feminization of poverty, women's needs remain largely invisible. Despite 20th century progress, women have not been able to make their material needs, as well as the household needs that they recognize better than most men, known to policy-makers—nor, certainly, to influence those who make law to reduce and eventually eradicate gender biases.

Against these odds, many women after Wollstonecraft will be remembered for extending the rights of well over half the human race. They rallied in the streets and brought other organised pressures to bear for universal adult franchise under their respective constitutions in most countries and used their hard-won political rights on behalf of other population sectors. Twentieth century women served as presidents, prime ministers,

ministers, members of parliaments, heads of parties, and judges in supreme courts. The demand for women's equality has gone forward from changing the laws to insisting that they be implemented for women's equality with men. Individually and collectively, women have enlarged their advocacy efforts beyond their local, national, and regional boundaries to the international forums. At no time in history have women organised themselves into such forceful non-governmental pressure groups and networks as in the last decade of the 20th century. And, moving into the corridors of power, they have moved power out into wider political spaces towards the realisation of full democracy.

Women's Agency in Governance: Early Indications

Recent indicators of women's agency range from raising consciousness of women's issues to changing institutional structures and processes and influencing the governance discourse in itself. Although there are expectations on women politicians to advance the gender agenda while in office, they do not necessarily do so. They usually cannot. In most cases, their numbers have not yet reached the necessary critical mass. Even when critical mass has been attained, critical alliances must be sought and cemented. The Ugandan experience showed that women politicians had more impact working in teams rather than individually, and in parliamentary committees rather than in plenary.

However, a few practical experiences from developing countries point to signal achievements. Some are recounted in later chapters of this collection.

Raising Consciousness of Women's Issues

Chapter 7 summarises the successes attained by the Ugandan Women's Caucus. Their first step was ensuring that their country's 1994 Constitution prohibits laws, traditions, and customs that undermine the dignity and well-being of women. This in itself was a transformative action for Ugandan political culture. The Caucus then lobbied for the establishment of an Equal Opportunities Commission to guarantee the Constitutional provisions for gender equality. Finally, in concert with other groups, these women enlarged the political scope of affirmative action in Uganda: women are now guaranteed 14 per cent of the Parliamentary seats and a third of the seats in local government.

---

[8] Ibid. See the chapter on Women's Agency and Social Change.
[9] In this connection, it should be noted that even in the United States, until the 1970s, married women could not obtain credit without the consent of their husbands.

Transforming the Political Agenda to Encompass Issues Important to Women

In Bhopal, India, the last of four women rulers introduced compulsory education for girls throughout their kingdom. This contributed to Bhopal having universal education for girls to this date. Nation-wide, the presence of a chairwoman on the Indian University Grants Commission was critical in a marked increase in women's accessing grants. In addition, India is also one of the few countries in which women parliamentarians have succeeded in persuading their fellow parliamentarians during the budgetary hearings to set a target of 30 per cent for women in the earmarking of total development funds—an achievement that parallels the South African Women's Budget Initiative documented by chapter 6 of this volume.

In Uganda, the Women's Caucus in Parliament succeeded in increasing the government's budget allocations for nutrition and for childhood development projects.

Similarly, in the Philippines, committed women parliamentarians introduced the very principle of targeted budget allocations for women and achieved an initial rate of 5 per cent. In 1998, their efforts also led to the adoption of a bill on rape.

Legislation Meaningful to Women's Lives

Again in Uganda, women introduced the issue of women's equity into the overall land reform bill. Kenyan women have repeatedly striven, inside and outside Parliament, to persuade the government to give women title to land and to establish bank accounts in their own name without the approval of their fathers or husbands. In Jamaica, women parliamentarians have helped set up a number of special funds, detailed in chapter 11, that directly or indirectly benefit women.

The *interpretation* of law is equally important. Most observers credit the new force of sexual harassment law throughout the USA to the presence of two women Justices on the nine-member Supreme Court, who mobilized their colleagues into considering a case, even in a primary school. In that country, legislation on sexual harassment is an issue left to the each of the 50 states (as is capital punishment and most education and health matters).

Women's Impact on Corruption

As noted in the Overview chapter of this volume, a recent World Bank study indicates a close correlation between women's representation in parliaments and a decrease in the incidence of corruption. If the findings of this initial 1999 inquiry, "Are Women Really the 'Fairer' Sex",[10] is borne out by further study, the implications are immense for women's entry into politics, as well as for government efficiency.

Women's Networking for Regional Learning and Co-operation

From the 1992 Earth Summit on, women caucused formally or informally at all the major UN conferences of the 1990s. Many took this experience back to the national level in structures ranging from parliaments through municipal assemblies—Uganda being only one example, which has had its own ripple effect throughout Sub-Saharan Africa. Similarly women's regional and international networks disseminated knowledge of the South African Women's Budget. This initiative is being replicated as far from that country as Barbados.

Changing Institutional Structures and Processes

Again in South Africa, women parliamentarians—together with civil society representatives and committed individuals—changed that country's electoral college system (including its competency requirements) to broaden the access of women to electoral posts. Similar movements are underway in countries as different as Botswana and Uruguay.

Influencing the Discourse of Governance Itself

The word "empowerment" in contemporary political parlance is very closely associated with the international women's movement. The impact of feminist language—including gender-neutral terminology—is also increasingly evident in the media and in legislation at all levels, including the international. Finally, as chapter 7 on gender violence shows, the definitions of "public" and "private" are changing throughout the world.

[10] David Dollar, Raymond Fisman and Roberta Gatti, *Are Women Really the Fairer Sex? Corruption and Women in Government*, Policy Research Report on Gender and Development, Working Paper Series No. 4, Development Economics Research Group, the World Bank, Washington DC, 1999.

WOMEN'S AGENCY IN GOVERNANCE

Key Challenges in Women's Agency

Despite all these remarkable advances, the 21st century opens with over one hundred million women missing in the world's population—as Sen himself pointed out in 1990.[11] We do not know how many thousands were aborted before birth, especially in South and East Asia, as a result of medical progress in identifying the sex of the foetus. This single ominous development of recent years points to the ferocity of preference for males that has dominated human history. We can hardly estimate the number of girls killed at birth or in childhood because of preferential nutrition and general care for their brothers over the millennia, let alone the 20th century denial of inoculation to girls against the major child-killers and other crippling or fatal diseases. The successive economic upheavals of the 20th century have accelerated the feminization of poverty in many countries, both developed and developing, in particular the unprecedented pace of globalisation during the last decade. In addition, war and civil strife now victimize civilian populations—with their majority of women—as never before. Beyond the industrialisation of war introduced by mass bombing in the First and Second World Wars, "ethnic cleansing", with gender-based atrocities, has become a military strategy and tool practiced from Bosnia to Rwanda to the guerrilla battlefields of Latin America.[12] Nonetheless, none of these phenomena is essentially new. Women's political participation is.

The "Mainstreaming" Debate

Paradoxically, a major question of women's agency in governance has arisen around the issue of *mainstreaming*—whether to join traditional political and other institutions or to change them by remaining outside their structures and the manifold relationships of those structures. This matter of choice—the free exercise of agency—has become almost an ideological divide in a number of countries and cultures.

The late Bella Abzug was quoted as stating that "mainstreaming is not about joining the polluted stream, but rather finding fresh new streams." During the 20th century, women the world over have often viewed mainstream politics as polluted—mired in corruption, hopelessly divided by class and ethnic interests, and frequently criminalised. In addition, many women have found that engaging in the political process requires money, muscle, exposure to hostile media and the adoption of male norms of behaviour, both aggressive and adversarial. In this connection, it is interesting to note that a 1999 World Bank study states that in a number of countries, a correlation exists between increasing women's representation in parliaments and decreasing incidence of corruption.[13]

During India's long struggle for Independence, Mohandas Gandhi's call upon Indians to address themselves to society rather than the state may well have increased the number of his followers among women. Despite his plea for their direct governmental participation once independence had been won, most politically active women in India had rooted their leadership in civil society roles rather than vying for seats in Parliament and other state positions. World-wide, women's historic exclusion from the hierarchical structures of the state may have directed them to exercising their agency in spheres of influence rather than in public political arenas.

Yet in India, too, it is women's political participation in local government structures that has led to perceiving women's political leadership as different from that of men. As the Indian feminist Devaki Jain recently remarked about the 1994 Panchayati raj (PRI) "revolution":

> "Some of the ways in which women, through PRI, are changing governance are evident in the issues they choose to tackle: water, alcohol abuse, education, health, and domestic violence. Women also express different values. Women value proximity, whether it be to a drinking water source, a fuel source, a crèche, a health centre, a court of justice or an office of administration. The enormous expansion of women in decentralised governance structures has highlighted the advantage of proximity, namely the redress of grievance and (most important of all, the ability to mobilize struggle at a local level where it is most meaningful …"[14]

[11] Amartya Sen, "More than 100 Million Women Are Missing", *The New York Review of Books*, 37:20, 20 December 1990.

[12] Charlotte Bunch and Niamh Reilly, *Demanding Accountability: The Global Campaign and Vienna Tribunal for Women's Human Rights*. Centre for Women's Leadership, Rutgers University, New Jersey and UNIFEM, New York, 1994.

[13] Op.cit. David Dollar, Raymond Fisman and Roberta Gatti.

[14] Devaki Jain, *Panchayat Raj: Women Changing Governance*, Gender in Development Monograph Series No. 5, UNDP, New York, 1996.

WOMEN'S
POLITICAL
PARTICIPATION
AND GOOD
GOVERNANCE:
**21ST CENTURY
CHALLENGES**

10

Attaining Critical Mass

Whatever one's views on Jain's statement, the almost million women now in Indian local government assemblies were swept into public political life by an affirmative action measure (examined in far greater detail in a chapter 5 of this collection on PRI). Again, the concept of critical mass—30 per cent or more—emerges as central to women's agency in governance. The "mainstreaming" and "outsider" approaches do not really exclude each other. In practice, they are mutually supportive. One example is the transformation of work practices in the United States during the 1990s, women having established themselves well beyond critical mass in the mainstream (paid) labour force. Only then did the conflicting demands of home and work obligations push the private sector to begin introducing "family-friendly" policies—such as paternal leave, tele-commuting and flexi-time— to keep highly trained and educated women in both the professions and other paid occupations that demand high levels of specialised skill. We will have to continue looking at numbers time and again in appraising gains in women's agency, particularly in governance.

Misperceptions of Women's Political Participation

Because most efforts to increase women's participation in politics have concentrated on enabling gender equality throughout society as a whole, this issue still tends to be perceived as a women's question rather than as an essential human concern—moreover, a matter vital to the survival of democracy. Consequently, one must look at a great number of factors that contribute to building women's agency in politics, whether or not they initially appear to constitute governance issues. The approaches listed below are by no means exhaustive, but provide a framework for concomitant strategies to achieve gender balance early in the 21st century.

Suggested Strategies for Women's Agency: a Possible Framework

I. PUBLIC ACTION

A *time frame* for achieving gender balance in political representation by 2010 must be formulated. Without time-bound goals, governments, political parties, lobbyists and women's groups cannot be held accountable.

Affirmative Action in Legislative Bodies

Justice delayed is justice denied. Ironically, this American legal adage has long been accepted for individuals indicted on criminal charges, but not for the female half of any country's population. Affirmative action in the political realm is a temporary measure required to attain long-belated justice to women economically and socially in the private as well as public realms. The general minimum target of 30 to 33 1/3 per cent is no more than critical mass. This is far from equality. It is arguable even as equity.[15]

In respect of affirmative action, it is worth noting the careful language of the 1979 Convention on the Elimination of All Forms of Discrimination against Women:

> *"Adoption by States Parties of temporary measures aimed at accelerating de facto equality between men and women shall not be considered discrimination, but shall in no way entail as a consequence the maintenance of unequal or separate standards; these measures shall be discontinued when the objectives of equality of opportunity and treatment have been achieved" (Article 4).*

Political Party and Electoral System Reform

The party system, so long a beneficiary of women's work from the ward level upwards, has long been an impediment to women's political leadership. In addition to affirmative action at the legislative level, political parties should honour commitments to *equality* and ensure that women *constitute fifty per cent of party membership, leadership, committee officers and candidates.*

For the moment, in Jamaica, where the Secretary-General of the ruling party is a woman, women

---

15 In Argentina, a quota adopted for Parliament in 1991 led in 1993 to an increase of women MPs to 28.4 per cent, a rise of 13.2 per cent over the prior level. In 1996, Marcela Bordenave of the Argentine Parliament credited this increase with the adoption of new legislation on a number of issues that Parliament had not hitherto considered, ranging from reproductive health to retirement. In the Parliament of Bangladesh, only 30 seats out of 330 are now reserved for women candidates—who are indirectly elected by the majority part members; in 1999, only seven women MPs were directly elected, despite the fact that there were three women ministers and one state ministers in the country's executive. The same type of inequitable pattern is manifest in Senegal, where a women heads the ruling socialist party and five of the 29 Cabinet ministers are women. Nonetheless, the Senegalese Parliament numbered only 19 women among its 540 deputies.

also serve as Speaker of the House, President of the Senate, Leader of Government Business and Majority Whip. It is also true that women slightly outnumber men in Jamaica. But this is the case in many other countries as well—and in most, no woman occupies any party or political post of any significance.

Party and electoral system reform have proved an effective tool for increasing women's agency in countries with widely different cultures. In South Africa, after changes to the law concerning party lists, women constituted 27 per cent of Parliament. In India, three parties headed by women—including the Congress Party that for so long dominated the country—have adopted a quota of one third for the nomination of women candidates. Across the globe in Chile, the Democracy Party, with a woman Vice-President, has adopted a rule whereby neither gender can have more than 60 per cent representation. And in Yemen, an emerging democracy, a constitutional amendment provides for a list system by which parties must nominate women candidates. Although only two of the 301 Yemeni MPs are currently women, this represents a step forward. The number of women judges in that country has now reached 44.

2. ACTION BY WOMEN'S ORGANISATIONS

Training in Information Technology

Countless studies, including several of the papers in this compilation, have underscored the importance of increasing women's agency by overcoming gender gaps in access to information technology. A number of international organisations, such as the Inter-parliamentary Union (IPU), have high-lighted the point, devoting particular attention to improving the access of women parliamentarians to information on IPU web sites and their linkages in cyber space. Women's organisations play a particularly important role in taking advantage of the new technologies. They seem to flourish in the borderless environment where civil society groups once previously ignored have attained a greater voice in governance. In so doing—as Wolfgang Reineke of the World Bank has recently pointed

out with regard to groups concerned with issues such as environment, agriculture, health and water world-wide[16]—women's organisations can overcome a number of the bureaucratic and other hierarchical conditions that hamper policy-makers in traditional institutions.

Development of Training Strategies for Increasing Women's Political Participation in the Following Areas:

- advocacy in gender awareness in politics
- capacity-building through networking
- negotiation skills;
- management;
- constituency-building;
- budget analysis;
- gender mainstreaming skills;
- use of mass media;
- political and voter education;
- mass mobilisation;
- long-term strategies for engaging younger generations.

3. ESTABLISHMENT OF ALLIANCES

Experiences in India, South Africa and Uganda, as well as a number of industrialised countries, point to the importance of building alliances between the various actors in local government, national government, the private sector and civil society to improve women's political participation. The alliance-building process requires partners to operate together on different issues in different spheres of governance. The role of the state is to enhance policies, such as affirmative action, for reaching gender balance in governmental structures. Civil society's strength lies in providing measures that will improve the quality of women's political participation such as training, lobby and outreach. And both influence the private sector—in which women appear poised to enter corporate senior management.[17] Perhaps more important, women world-wide are establishing more and more small and medium-size enterprises, especially in the retail and service trades, where start-up costs are lower than in manufacturing and other businesses and where e-commerce offers particular advantages.[18]

WOMEN'S
POLITICAL
PARTICIPATION
AND GOOD
GOVERNANCE:
21ST CENTURY
CHALLENGES

---

[16] Wolfgang H. Reineke, "The Other World Wide Web: Global Public Policy Networks", *Foreign Policy*, No. 117, Winter 1999 - 2000
[17] Marina Fanning, "Bridging the Gender Gap in Today's Organisations: Understanding the Cultural Differences of Gender", *Management Systems International*, Washington DC, 1995.
[18] See "Women and Decision-Making", *Women 2000*, United Nations, New York, October 1997.

In almost all countries there is also a need to create more positive relations between politicians and civil society and an exchange between women in different substantive spheres to shape complementary strategies. In addition, engagement with religious groups is required to address gender inequities debates with religious hierarchies, particularly where sacred texts are interpreted to inhibit women's potential participation.

All in all, alliance building serves as an effective mechanism for:

■ exchanging information on women's experience in identifying the conditions necessary to create sustainable linkages among different governance actors;

■ dialogue among all these actors to increase the impact of women's political participation; and

■ establishing accountability towards women in different constituencies.

4. ROLE MODELS

Special collaborative, alliance-building efforts are needed to change perceptions concerning women's leadership, particularly by validating women's leadership to the women-in-the-street (and on the small farmstead) as credible, effective, and better than men's on a variety of issues. The average woman needs to know that women leaders, like themselves, have to juggle responsibilities and priorities in the public and private worlds—that the leader is also a parent and homemaker like the woman who operates a market stall or factory sewing machine. The human person, female or male, plays different roles at different times. Women still tend to appreciate their contribution in their private and unpaid roles more than men do, in aspects relating to social maintenance.

The role of the mass *news* media is particularly crucial. Proactive and continuous dialogue between women leaders and women's lobbies with the news media is needed not only for highlighting women's leadership, but for the coverage of issues particularly important to redressing gender inequities. These range from areas as diverse as early marriage

and health research allocations. To take another example, the increasing news attention to national and international drug trafficking should feature not only the negative impacts of these illegal trades on women and their agency (as distinct from welfare), but their diversion of funding from vital development concerns.[19]

5. TARGETING YOUNG WOMEN

It is appropriate to conclude this chapter by observing that most development and political participation activities still target adult women. Yet in attempting to leapfrog a gender bias heritage of millennia, one cannot forget the primacy of early conditioning and training. "The child is father to the man," remarked the English poet William Wordsworth. "Give me the child until the age of six," said the Jesuit educator Ignatius Loyola, "and I shall show you the man." Both injunctions apply equally to girls. Unless their political education, and agency, starts before women are encumbered by their other roles—care-giving in the home and economic activity, paid or unpaid, inside or outside the home—the transformation of political systems will take perhaps another century, if not another millennium.

BIBLIOGRAPHY
Bunch, Charlotte and N. Reilly (1994). *Demanding Accountability: The Global Campaign and Vienna Tribunal for Women's Human Rights.* Centre for Women's Leadership, Rutgers University, New Jersey and UNIFEM, New York.
Dollar, D., R. Fisman, and R. Gatti (1999). *Are Women Really the Fairer Sex? Corruption and Women in Government,* Policy Research Report on Gender and Development, Working Paper Series No. 4, Development Economics Research Group, the World Bank, Washington DC.
Fanning, Marina (1995). "Bridging the Gender Gap in Today's Organisations: Understanding the Cultural Differences of Gender", *Management Systems International,* Washington DC, 1995.
Gallagher, Margaret (1995). *An Unfinished Story,* UNESCO, Paris.
Jain, Devaki (1996). *Panchayat Raj: Women Changing Governance,* Gender in Development Monograph Series No. 5, UNDP, New York.
Krug, Barbara and I. van Staveren (1999). "Gender Audit: Whim or Voice" paper to be published in *Public Finance and Management,* Internet journal at website http://www.spaef.com/, Rotterdam.
Mehlomakhulu, Sandra (1999). *Creating New Structures of a Chapter: Gender and Corruption,* paper presented at the Transparency International Annual Meting, Durban, South Africa, October 1999, Transparency International Zimbabwe.
Reineke, Wolfgang H (1999). "The Other World Wide Web: Global Public Policy Networks", *Foreign Policy,* No. 117, Winter 1999—2000.
Sen, Amartya (1990). "More than 100 Million Women Are Missing", *The New York Review of Books,* 37:20, 20 December issue.
_____(1999). *Development as Freedom,* Alfred A. Knopf, New York.
United Nations (1997) Women and Decision-Making", *Women 2000,* New York, October.

WOMEN'S
AGENCY IN
GOVERNANCE

---

[19] As Margaret Gallagher has pointed out in the UNESCO survey, *An Unfinished Story* (Paris, 1995), women can change a number of the ways in which well-established issues are covered.

CHAPTER 3

BEIJING + 5: WOMEN'S POLITICAL PARTICIPATION: REVIEW OF STRATEGIES AND TRENDS

AZZA KARAM[20]

On the eve of the 21st century, more than a hundred years after women finally attained the franchise in New Zealand, the first of all countries to recognize this inalienable right, the question of women's political participation has become permanently inscribed on the international agenda and permeates many regional and national plans of action. In 1995, when the Fourth World Conference on Women adopted the Beijing Platform for Action, 10 per cent of the members of national legislative bodies world-wide were women. Today, the per centage has gone up to 12 per cent. An increase of 2 per cent over a period of five years may appear infinitesimal. But when climbing a steep precipice, arriving at higher plateau is no small achievement.

Whether political, social, economic or cultural, the rights women have achieved over the last 100 years and more have hardly been given, but hard-fought and hard-won. Even when men presided over the ultimate authority and decision-making structures, it was women who expressed, formulated, lobbied, and sometimes simply protested their rights into place.

Alluding to Virginia Wolf in *A Room of One's Own*, Alida Brill states that the mirror women have so long held up to men—a mirror that exaggerates and flatters male attributes—has increasingly projected a more realistic image since women's entry into public life. However, she cautions, many men resent these newer projections and therefore fight against them.[21] Some argue that in many cases, women politicians have become "just like other men" in their attitudes—usually meaning aggressive, manipulative, unfair or any of a number of pejorative adjectives. Others contend that many women in public life have studiously avoided taking up issues particularly (but by no means only) relevant to women's welfare or interests. Brill therefore asks again: "Is there a woman's voice in politics which is unique? Does it really make a difference that women have achieved political office? Would it be just as good if there were more men in politics world-wide who were sympathetic to the women's agenda?"

BEIJING + 5:
WOMEN'S
POLITICAL
PARTICIPATION:
REVIEW OF
STRATEGIES
AND TRENDS

---

[20] Azza Karam is Middle East Programme Director at the Queens University of Belfast, Belfast, Northern Ireland, United Kingdom.

[22] Brill, Alida, ed. 1995. *A Rising Public Voice: Women in Politics Worldwide.* New York: The Feminist Press. p.1.

She answers by insisting " … without our own voices being heard inside the government arena and halls of public policy and debate, we are without the right of accountability - a basic entitlement of those who are governed". She subsequently argues, like many others, that women's presence in the political arena has changed the nature of the political agenda itself. Questions concerning reproductive health and choice, nutrition, equality in education and in employment opportunities and circumstances, child care and related 'family-friendly'[23] aspects, and environment are only a few the areas that women have either brought into public debate or highlighted with significant substantive victories at both national and international levels.[24]

Nelson and Chowdhury, among others, take this point further by specifying two dimensions that are crucial to considerations of any international endeavour:

■ in addition to the issues mentioned above—many of them erroneously perceived as women-specific—women actually consider all broader social and political concerns within their political interests and mandate; and

■ many commonalties exist between concerns considered crucial by women, regardless of their geo-political and socio-economic situations. Nelson and Chowdhury cite violence against women and economic participation in particular.

This latter dimension is significant because it indicates that all societies share difficulties in achieving comprehensive gender-fair changes. It also underlines the power of women as a "mobilizing force".[25]

Two other important features of women's entry into politics are highlighted Nelson and Chowdhury, as well as the United Nations Development Programme (UNDP) *Human Development Report 1995: Gender and Development:*[26]

In no society do women enjoy the same opportunities as men; and

Removing gender inequality has nothing to do with national income or wealth.

Assessing progress since the adoption of the Beijing Platform for Action is no easy task and requires looking into the present and the future simultaneously. This paper is structured along the following lines:

■ A review of the main recommendations made in the Platform for Action;

■ A review of trends in women's participation since its adoption in 1995;

■ Key recommendations of major international conferences on governance that have since taken place;

■ An overview of the challenges women face in attaining *de jure* equality in the 21st century;

■ Good governance practices to enhance and deepen building women's constituencies—lessons learned and future steps.

Recommendations for Action in the Beijing Platform for Action

…[W]omen's equal participation in political life plays a pivotal role in the general process of the advancement of women. Women's equal participation in decision-making is not only a demand for simple justice or democracy but can also be seen as a necessary condition for women's interests to be taken into account. Without the active participation of women and the incorporation of women's perspectives at all levels of decision-making, the goals of equality, development and peace cannot be achieved."

Thus begins the Platform's section on *Women in Power and Decision-Making.*[27]

WOMEN'S
POLITICAL
PARTICIPATION
AND GOOD
GOVERNANCE:
21ST CENTURY
CHALLENGES

---

[23] Family-friendly policies are those which facilitate for both women and men to combine employment in the job market with their respective family commitments (e.g. parental leave, reproductive rights, etc.). Hege Skjeie refers to this when she talks about 'the politics of care' in Norway, and how women's presence in politics impacts on these issues. For more detail, see Hege Skjeie, 1998. "Credo on Difference: Women in Parliament in Norway" in, Azza Karam, ed. *Women in Parliament: Beyond Numbers.* Stockholm: International IDEA. pp.183-190.

[24] Ergo the various international meetings, declarations and conventions around many of these aspects: the Convention for the Elimination of All Forms of Discrimination against Women (CEDAW), in addition to what occurred as a result of international meetings in Rio in 1990 (environment), Cairo in 1994 (population), Beijing in 1995 (women), and Stockholm in 1996 (children), to name but a few.

[25] Nelson, Barbara and Najma Chowdhury, "Redefining Politics: Patterns of Women's Political Engagement from a Global Perspective", in Barbara Nelson and Najma Chowdhury, eds. 1994. *Women and Politics Worldwide,* New Haven and London: Yale University Press. pp.10-11.

[26] UNDP, 1995. *Human Development Report 1995: Gender and Development.* Oxford: Oxford University Press. Much of the information quoted here was obtained from the Internet copy, and thus page numbers are inapplicable.

[27] See Annex 2 for full text.

Some of the recommendations of the Platform can be summarized as follows:

■ Setting a firm timetable to end all manner of legal discrimination against women (along the lines of CEDAW), as well as establishing a framework to promote legal equality;

■ Initiating specific measures targeted to acquiring a short-term threshold of 30 per cent for women in national decision-making positions, with a long-term aim of 50 per cent;

■ Mobilizing national and international efforts to facilitate for everyone—and for women in particular—greater access to economic and political opportunities.

The Beijing Platform for Action advocates institutional mechanisms in the form of national machinery to focus on mainstreaming (integrating at all levels) gender concerns within national policy, creating the conditions for gender equality at all levels, and allocating specific national and international resources towards these ends. The Platform embodies two strategic objectives:

■ ensuring women's equal access to and full participation in power structures and decision-making; and

■ increasing women's capacity to participate in decision-making and leadership.

The recommendations are thus specifically directed to governments, political parties, the United Nations (UN), and civil society.

The United Nations is one of the organisations in which much hope is invested and which has consistently been the motor for ensuring the gender issue is on the global agenda in a number of ways. However, the Organisation has had to struggle with problems of credibility and efficiency, particularly in implementing its recommendations.[28] This underlines the importance of working in partnership with a wide array, not only of institutions, but also of objectives and visions—the more so in this era of economic globalisation, in which so much power has moved from governments into the marketplace.

---

[28] See Marilee Karl, 1995. pp. 67-68.

It is important to note that equality and enhancement are not necessarily one and the same goal. In many countries, the vast majority of men lack significant social, economic, and political powers. Thus far, priority does go to gender-equality policies: this enterprise is difficult enough. However, we should not concentrate on equality in numbers at the expense of more strategic objectives, such as *enhancing* the performance of those women already in decision-making positions. This is not to say that women's performance should be monitored more closely than men's or those expectations of women should be higher. Nor does it negate the target of 30 per cent. But it must be remembered that the political sphere has usually slighted roles traditionally assigned to women, notably family and household management and has therefore ignored the need of most women in politics to balance time between their new responsibilities and those dictated by the vast majority of cultures. Geared to a context of male lifestyles, political arenas provide their lessons within it—at the simplest level, excluding women from bars and any number of clubs and other spaces that serve as caucuses. Even where such barriers have dropped, women are relatively late entrants to politics and could benefit immensely from systematized methods of exchanging experiences with veterans, both male and female. This is probably as critical to political impact as the 30 per cent threshold. In addition, the time has now come to also look at *how* women are making an impact, what their needs are—from local councils to the office of national president or prime minister—and what mechanisms already in use, have been shown to be powerful, effective and different.

Trends in Women's Participation Since 1995: Figures and the Facts They May Obscure

THE FIGURES

The number of women heads of state or government (excluding queens) now totals six, four of whom came to power after 1995—in Bangladesh (Prime Minister since June 1996), Guyana (President since 1997), Ireland (President since 1997) and Sri Lanka, where a mother and daughter are, respectively, President and Prime Minister. According to the Inter-Parliamentary Union (IPU) statistics, from 1945 to 1995 the per centage of women MPs worldwide has increased fourfold. Their latest statistics indicate that, in 1998, the world average of women in parliaments (both houses combined) is 12.7 per cent, with the highest in the Nordic countries (37.6 per cent), followed by the Americas (15.5 per cent), Asia (13.4 per cent), Europe OSCE member countries (excluding the Nordic countries) (12.5 per cent), sub-Saharan Africa (11.6 per cent) the Pacific (8.3 per cent) and, last, the Arab states (3.3 per cent). In addition, since 1995, six countries elected a woman speaker of parliament for the first time: Ethiopia (1995), Latvia (1995), Peru (1995), Jamaica (1996), Malta (1996) and Poland (1997).

According to the United Nations Division for the Advancement of Women (UN/DAW) *Fact Sheet on Women in Government* of 1996, the per centage of women in both ministerial and sub-ministerial levels ranges from zero (in about 15 countries[29]), to 30 per cent in two countries as distant and dissimilar as the Bahamas and Sweden. However, of the 15 countries with no women in government positions in 1996, eight were Arab states.

Statistical data on women in important judicial positions is difficult to obtain even at the level of the highest court. World-wide statistics are therefore largely meaningless; the fact that Nigeria has not published its data for a number of years simply masks the fact that a number of women serve on that country's highest tribunals. To take the United States Supreme Court as an example, two of the current nine Justices are women—but this has not changed since 1995. And of the 1,181 federal judges in the USA, only 154 are women.

All these facts taken together are particularly ironic, since in both ancient Egypt and the West, justice has been symbolized by women—in the West, usually blindfolded to signify absolute impartiality. Yet since most law world-wide usually works in favour of men, however gender-blind or gender-neutral it may appear, the need for a gender perspective in the judiciary is critical, if only because laws and their interpretation and implementation often affect women and men differently.

In its study on women in local governments in different regions of the world, the International Union of Local Authorities (IULA) sets a represen-tation rate of no more than 60 per cent for either gender—in short, a minimum target of 40 per cent for women. Although the IULA succeeds in bringing together far more data than that available on women in judiciaries, its information remains uneven.[30] Nonetheless, existing statistics indicate that women's political participation at the local level generally surpasses national trends. This has certainly been the case in the West, where women's participation in community politics has long been viewed as an extension of their traditional involvement in household management. Current trends towards devolution may make holding local office far more powerful and prestigious than it has hitherto been—a development that may also favour women because so many still shoulder disproportionate responsibilities for household management that preclude their leaving home for remote capitals.

In Africa, women's membership in local councils is estimated at probably less than 5 per cent.[31] Statistically, the Eastern Mediterranean and the Middle East furnished no information, except for Turkey. There, 0.46 per cent of mayors in the 1994 municipal elections emerged as chief executives of districts, none as the head of an entire municipality. Although the IULA provides no general data for Asia, it calls attention to the Panchayati raj Institutions experiment in India that began with a Constitutional amendment in 1992 (discussed in an extensive case study later in this volume) that reserves 33 per cent of the seats in local decision-making bodies (both urban and rural) to women. While Filipino women are increasing their membership in local councils, particularly in the rural areas, the number of women local representatives in Australia dropped after their last council elections of 1997. Again, as the *Human Development Report 1995* indicates, gender activity rates in politics, as in other areas, appears to have little to do with national income or wealth.

Europe, Latin America, North America and the Caribbean provided more statistical data, which can be summarized as follows:

Europe: In the European Union in 1997, one out of five local elected representatives was female, with the situation varying from one country to another. In Sweden, 40 per cent of Local Assemblies seats were held by women, as compared with less than 4 per cent in Greece.[32]

---

[29] These are: Afghanistan, Bahrain, Djibouti, Lebanon, Monaco, Myanmar, Nauru, Nepal, Saudi Arabia, the Solomon Islands, Somalia, the United Arab Emirates and Yemen.
[30] All statistical information obtained from IULA, 1998. *Women in Local Government.* Stockholm, pp. 18-28.
[31] IULA, 1998. p.18.
[32] IULA, 1998. p.25.

Latin America: Data compiled between 1992 and 1995 (after which, data is scant) showed an average rate for women of 7.5 per cent for mayors and 3.8 per cent for municipal councilors.

North America: USA figures from 1990 indicate an average figure of 17 per cent for women mayors and 23 per cent for women in local councils. Other statistics reveal that in January 1997, 12 of the nation's 100 largest cities had women mayors or city managers,[33] and in March 1997, that 202 of the 975 US cities with more than 30,000 residents had women mayors.[34]

In Canada, 18 per cent of council members are women. In Quebec, a quota to equalize the number of seats for women and men resulted in an increase in the per centage of women mayors and councilors between 1985 and 1996, but a decline thereafter. IULA also observes that in Quebec and Montreal in particular, connections to the local women's movement played a key role in inspiring women to run for election.[35]

The Caribbean: Trinidad and Tobago follows the pattern of higher female representation at the local level in comparison with the national: 21 per cent in local councils and 14 per cent at the mayoral positions.[36]

Since 1995, both the number and level of women in decision-making has increased in the United Nations itself. For the first time a female Deputy Secretary-General was appointed, and for the first time, both the United Nations High Commissioner for Refugees and the World Health Organisation have been headed by women. These recent additions bring the total of women executive heads to five organisations—the others being UNICEF, the UN Population Fund and the World Food Programme.

However, in non-governmental organisations (NGOs), we lack figures on women who are executive heads, even in those that deal; primarily with political participation. Such information is now vital because NGOs have been playing increasingly influential roles at the heart of civil societies across the world, in many instances stepping into the political, social and economic vacuums left by failed and failing states. Women's NGOs, for instance, have been significant actors in brokering peace agreements in countries torn by civil strife.

THE FACTS

Given the available data, uneven as it may be, the following trends emerge:

Governments:

■ Despite the fact that many governments have adopted affirmative action measures and the rhetoric of gender balance, the threshold of 30 per cent advocated by the Human Development Report 1995, as a prelude to the 50 per cent that would reflect women's true global population position, remains remote in most of the world.

■ In some countries, such as those of the Arab region, freedom of association remains a politically sensitive issue because of the predominance of authoritarian regimes alone—quite apart from the human rights principle of the equal rights of men and women to engage in political activities. Indeed, women's organisations encounter particular difficulties in the rising tensions between some governments and political Islamic groups (Islamists).[37]

■ Although differences in electoral systems appear to have marked impact on women's representation, the information collected thus far remains so heavily European and/or western,[38] that it is difficult to advocate any specific electoral system as promoting women's participation in politics.

■ Indeed, unless better-balanced information emerges on women in general and gendered statistics in particular, it is difficult to establish effective mechanisms to monitor women's access to senior levels of decision-making. A concerted international effort for data collection is therefore necessary.

---

[33] Source: Bureau of the Census, U.S. Department of Commerce, as reported on the Internet.
[34] Source: Center for the American Woman and Politics (compiled using the United States Conference of Mayors January 1997 directory), as reported on the Internet.
[35] IULA, 1998. p. 28.
[36] IULA, 1998. p. 28.
[37] See Azza Karam, 1998. *Women, Islamisms and the State.* London: Macmillan.
[38] For elaboration on the differential impact of electoral systems on women's representation, and for further references, see Richard Matland, 1998, "Enhancing Women's Political Participation: Legislative Recruitment and Electoral Systems", in Azza Karam, ed. the *International IDEA Handbook on Women in Parliament: Beyond Numbers.* Stockholm: International IDEA. pp. 65-90.

BEIJING + 5:
WOMEN'S
POLITICAL
PARTICIPATION:
REVIEW OF
STRATEGIES
AND TRENDS

Political Parties

- The number of women in parliaments and in local governments around the world indicates that political parties have some way to go putting gender-conscious policies on their agendas and implementing these within their ranks.

The United Nations

- The rise of women to prominent leadership positions within the UN system points to progress in this realm, as is the increase in UN collection, assessment and dissemination of information on women in decision-making. Nonetheless, efforts in the latter regard should be strengthened.

Civil Society

- Again, despite a growing wealth of anecdotal material, there remain grave shortcomings in systematic information collection. The rise in women's representation in community-based organisations in many countries world-wide, particularly during the last five years seems to indicate that women are increasingly seizing opportunities for political participation where they can balance these activities with their traditional household responsibilities. Whether this will lead to greater activism at the national level and/or significantly change national political agendas remains to be seen.

THE BEIJING PLATFORM FOR ACTION IN PRACTICE

The Fourth World Conference on Women spurred a debate on matters of direct concern to women well before, during and after the actual meeting in Beijing. Although the Platform for Action is not legally binding, its signature by a vast variety of governments has generated significant moral force and the substantive and technical framework outline for a wide spectrum of initiatives in countries as diverse as Colombia, Japan, and Turkey.[39] These have ranged from setting up special committees to pressure and monitor

governments in implementing the Platform as a whole to multiparty collaborations to lobby governments on specific issues. In Poland, such efforts led to the liberalisation of existing anti-abortion law, in Turkey to amending the civil code and in Peru to setting up a commission to modify laws pertaining to women in Congress.

Mobilisation and motivation for discussions and initiatives aside, women's participation—at the very least in terms of numbers—remains hampered as long as wide gaps in the rates of political participation between the two genders, particularly when the definition of a "political space" is broadened to include domains such as the business sector, and the academia. Even in Sweden, despite the fact that women constitute 44 per cent of MPs, they represent less than 10 per cent of senior academic staff and the decision-making echelons of the business community. By contrast, in Egypt, although women MPs hold less than 2 per cent of parliamentary seats, they occupy over 40 per cent of high academic chairs—but less than 10 per cent of executive positions in business. Although many African countries have witnessed little or no change, largely because of resource and management constraints, others, such as Uganda, South Africa and Kenya, are witnessing significant progress for women in position of power. However, Beijing appears to have had little impact for women politically in either Latin America or the Arab world, despite the vast differences between these two regions.

In this regard, it may be worth remarking that in sharing experience regions tend to compare themselves to the West and not to other developing countries. Latin America and the Middle East have many traits in common and might therefore profit immensely by sharing their respective experiences.

Affirmative action measures

Affirmative action measures, such as quotas and particular types of electoral systems (e.g. the proportional representation system) continue being used to rectify imbalances in political representation. However, the initial debacle on introducing quotas for women in the Indian Parliament—the bill was physically shredded before being tabled—indicates the aura of controversy that persists on the subject. Quotas are allegedly undemocratic because the women who benefit from them are (again, allegedly) not elected and are therefore unrepresentative. Others who oppose

WOMEN'S POLITICAL PARTICIPATION AND GOOD GOVERNANCE: 21ST CENTURY CHALLENGES

---

[39] Migirou, Kalliope. 1998. "Towards Effective Implementation of International Women's Human Rights Legislation", in Azza Karam, ed. *The International IDEA Handbook on Women in Parliament: Beyond Numbers* (Stockholm: International IDEA). pp. 201-214. The examples quoted ranged from setting up special committees to pressurise and monitor how governments implement the Beijing Platform for Action recommendations such as those in Japan, to taking up cross-party collaborative efforts to lobby governments on specific issues such as in Poland and Turkey.

quotas argue that they demean women by viewing them as undeserving and incapable of fulfilling the demands of the position; quota-women are by definition token figures, unlikely to use their new positions to effect real change.

Quotas usually become more popular when presented as "a helping hand" for women against the multiplicity of obstacles they traditionally face in trying to enter the political arena. Other quota proponents hold that no group, female or male, can truly represent another and that failure to assist the less privileged in obtaining an opportunity to perform is in itself unjust. In addition, quota advocates argue that such measures in any domain are temporary means of correcting imbalance; the fact that in the political arena they are now used predominantly for women merely indicates that such an imbalance exists.

Research on the effects of electoral systems on women's representation is so far sketchy and predominantly Western. Studies carried out in Australia, Canada, Germany, New Zealand, Norway, the United Kingdom, and the United States show a positive correlation between proportional representation (PR) systems and the number of women in the national legislature. Very few, if any, detailed and long-term studies on how electoral systems affect women's representation in the South are available.

In sum, we can conclude the following:

■ The Beijing Platform for Action is an important tool for those working on enhancing women's political participation. Many of its recommendations serve as reference points for plans of action world-wide at levels ranging from the international to the local.

■ With the exception of very few countries, women now occupy important political positions around the world, though the extent varies sharply from nation to another.

■ The number of women in government remains, however, far below the 30 per cent target specified by UNDP, despite significant progress.

■ Information and data, particularly gender desegregated data, while impressive on women in parliaments and government (ministerial and sub-ministerial) remains low and seriously uneven, particularly on aspects such as local

government and judiciaries, as well as NGOs and the private sector.

■ Affirmative action strategies still need to be implemented in some areas, especially in the developing countries of the world.

Recent International Conferences on Governance

In 1997, the Inter-Parliamentary Union (IPU) convened a conference entitled "Towards Partnership Between men and Women in Politics" in New Delhi (14–18 February), attended by parliamentary delegations from 80 countries, representatives of international parliamentary organisations, intergovernmental organisations and international NGOs. In July of that year, UNDP held an international conference in New York on "Governance for Sustainable Growth and Equity" that brought together more than 1000 ministers and other senior national officials from 147 countries, along with mayors and urban administrators, members of parliament, and representatives of civil society organisations. Women's political participation was a key feature of the agenda.

The IPU conference[40] issued the New Delhi Declaration of recommendations to improve women's political participation, ranging in subject matter from attitudes through training in a variety of areas to increase both the presence and participation of women in decision-making bodies locally, nationally, regionally and internationally. Reiterating the principles of women's rights as human rights, along with the critical mass target of 30 per cent, the Declaration also called upon political parties to facilitate the equal participation of both men and women, as well as to become more generally open to women's demands. Reserved seats were for political parties, as well as local and national representative institutions. The Conference also regarded proportional representation as the most promising approach for bringing women into decision-making forums.

Further, the Declaration emphasized the importance of women's education and political training, including the importance of facilitating campaign financing for women politicians; it therefore called for a

[40] Inter-Parliamentary Union. 1997. *Towards Partnership between Men and Women in Politics.* New Delhi (14-18 February). Series Reports and Documents No. 29. Geneva: Inter-Parliamentary Union.

compilation of a directory of world-wide institutions engaged in training with on these issues. It also underlined gender inequities in the labour market and the media and, in the latter regard, recommended an enhanced image of women politicians in the media to spur changes in traditional attitudes. The Declaration also stressed the need for setting up specialised national bodies and advisory boards, some within parliamentary structures as monitoring and advisory bodies. Last but not least, the Declaration stressed the need for international bodies to ensure gender-equal participation.

Structured in four simultaneous forums—respectively for senior national officials, mayors, parliamentarians and civil society organisations—the UNDP Conference on Governance for Sustainable Growth and Equity centred its gender recommendations on equalizing (increasing up to 50 per cent) women's representation at all levels of decision-making institutions and increasing the allocation of international resources for capacity-building to that effect. Another major recommendation stressed the need to remove obstacles to women's public participation and emphasized the responsibility of political parties in this regard, as well as that of civil society organisations, in ensuring the simultaneity of macro- and micro-level empowerment measures. The Conference also highlighted the need for mechanisms to translate recommendations to policies, as well as broadening the scope and themes of national social dialogues so as to include the concerns of media and academic circles.

Whereas the recommendations of the UNDP Conference tend to deal with the broader issues, those of the IPU examine of women's political engagement from the micro to the macro in detail, covering political parties, education, affirmative action, changing attitudes, training, parliaments, national commissions of women, international bodies, and directories of information—in short, the major challenges to women's political participation in the 21st century. The ensemble, however, reveals certain shortcomings, notably the following:

■ They do not sufficiently emphasize certain information gaps and how these can be rectified;

■ They do not argue strongly for comparative information-gathering to fill in not only gaps in data, but in qualitative areas, such as enhancing women's political contributions;

■ They still tend to skirt the debates concerning quotas and other affirmative action measures, and thereby neglect opportunities to gain insights into alternative forms of promoting women's participation in political life;

■ They maintain an overemphasis on numbers.[41]

Challenges Facing Women's *de Jure* Equality in the 21st Century

Although the very disparity between *de jure* and *de facto* situations is significant in all human rights issues, the letter of the law remains one of the most important empowering instruments for the achieving rights. Few of the challenges to women's *de jure* equality in the 21st century are really new. Many, however, have taken on a different face— among these, in our own time, the challenge of electronic communication technology, which has become a critical tool of freedom of expression as well as economic empowerment.

Challenges differ from one country and region to another, often within individual countries. Political corruption and ensuing fears are major challenges in many parts of the world. It is probably most useful to look at challenges by sphere, notably socio-cultural, economic and political.

Socio-cultural

Despite the massive social science literature that has accumulated around the term "culture", notably within the last decade, our purposes here require little more than assuming that culture is a set of attitudes, rarely static and often uncon-scious, many of them historically conditioned. These can be local, ethnic or national and even global, particularly with regard to gender and class concerns. They shape people's sense of identity and the ways in which they behave, either as individuals or in groups. Far from being consistent, they may clash, even within an individual. To take only one simplistic example, a woman may act in one context or at one particular point in time to champion the rights of women in general and subsequently as an advocate of certain class interests that militate against equality between the genders within the labour market.

---

[41] See Kathleen Staudt, 1989 "Women in High Level Political Decision-Making: A Global Analysis". pp.34-37.

Women in particular play multiple roles. In most countries, they are perceived as having "primary" responsibilities as wives and mothers for which they receive no overt remuneration. They may also enter the labour market, formal or informal, beyond the immediate household economy. A political career usually emerges as a second or third job.[42]

These perceptions are closely connected to a traditional understanding of space as private and public, women generally being relegated to the former, even to the exclusion of the latter. These notions are remarkably persistent and lie at the very heart of most of the difficulties women face not only entering politics, but achieving credibility and impact within this sphere. As Netumbo Nandi-Ndaiah, Namibia's Minister of Women's Affairs, remarked at the UNDP Conference on Governance for Sustainable Growth and Equity, "It is women who are managing day-to-day life in the family—making sure there is enough food for breakfast, for lunch, for dinner. Now if a woman is able to do this in her own family, why is she not able to ensure that the national cake is shared equally for the benefit of everybody? Because these are the skills that we would like to see in a good Minister of Finance."

The characterization of politics as "dirty" arises partly from the pervasive public/private dichotomy, which tends to posit the home or "private" space as a haven from stresses outside, the wife/mother figure guaranteeing harmony within an atmosphere of ultimate trust and inclusion. One example of this myth is the idealization of the mothers of Mafia members.

Even where they may possess considerable independent income, women in politics rely on a support network—and usually, the provision of a number of social services—based on family-friendly considerations that most countries lack, regardless of per capita GDP. Basic education constitutes another problem. According to the UNDP Human Development Report 1995, women outnumber men two to one among the developing world's 900,000 million illiterates and girls constitute the majority of the 130 million children without access to primary school. Further, because population growth has outstripped the expansion of women's education in many developing countries, the number of female illiterates has actually increased.[43]

---

[42] See Richard Matland, "The Effect of Development and Culture on Women's Representation", in Azza Karam, ed. 1998. *Women in Parliament: Beyond Numbers.* pp. 29.

[43] UNDP. *Human Development Report 1995*, obtained from Internet version.

Economic

As indicated at the beginning of this paper, economic and political development do not go hand in hand for women. The situation of a number of the oil-producing states is only the most glaring case in point. Even in Sweden, many women in politics suffer from entrenched, often subtle discriminatory attitudes. Nonetheless, poverty remains a major impediment largely because the daily struggle for survival precludes time for women's engaging in political activity. Worse still, poverty-stricken women do not yet seem to have benefited from women's entry into politics.

A number of women who might otherwise embark on political lives are discouraged by the lack of funds not only for financing electoral campaigns, but access to resources adequate to undertaking significant initiatives. These may entail extensive (and expensive) research, as well as outreach and public information efforts. A paradox of many of the strong recommendations made by international gatherings that both political parties and governments attempt to provide and/or set up funds for women in political life, is that women may end up confined to token funds, and possibly cut off from access to other resources.

Political

Research demonstrates that the type of electoral system plays an important role in determining whether or not women get properly involved on party lists or get elected—notably Proportional Representation. However, since most of the information available on this issue is specific to the Western world—and because each electoral system is affected by other cultural and economic considerations—no one particular system can be universally advocated.

In addition, because most powerful political parties reflecting the more general conditions in the rest of society, they do not easily accept or promote many women in their internal structures. Hence the current concerns being voiced about the viability and popularity of parties as vehicles for women's political advancement in the face of emerging alternative political entities, such as NGOs.

Moreover, lack of sufficient training and communication skills or media know-how remains a tremendous problem for women in developed and developing countries alike, particularly in this age of the media. The gravity of this issue is compounded by the fact that the media tend to feed on novelty. "Just being a woman politician is not enough to raise interest … we need a story that is interesting and would attract attention"[44] is not an uncommon view among media personnel in a number of countries, developing as well as developed.

Internet communications may well emerge as the determining variable in the years to come. Hence the importance of situating both women themselves and men with strong commitments to women's political advancement in institutions on the cusp of the newest communications systems. "Knowledge is power" is probably an even stronger injunction today than it was when the phrase came into wide circulation in 19th century Europe. Women who have limited access to common contemporary office facilities are at a distinct disadvantage in today's political world in terms of their capacity, efficiency and even local potential.

Good Governance Practices to Enhance and Deepen Building Women's Constituencies and Future Steps

Good Governance Practices

While no blueprints are universally valid, some practices appear to have had success in most parts of the world. Those that have been tried and tested at various levels can be summarized as follows:

- gender-balanced representation within political parties and all other public institutions;

- setting up of specialised national machinery for monitoring, implementing and, when necessary, creating gender equality policies;

- setting up a woman's budget targeted to provide funds to secure gender equality measures and assist women in their political careers (e.g. campaign financing);

- mainstreaming gender concerns at all levels of society, starting with poverty-alleviation;

- adoption and implementation of affirmative action measures wherever there is a perceived

need, even in areas that appear to have little relevance to politics;[45]

- adjusting the discourse so as to emphasize the sharing of responsibilities rather than power takeovers;

- Comparing, comparing and comparing yet again experiences strategies and mechanisms from around the world.

Other lessons that remain to be formulated and implemented as practices are the following:

- assessing impact in terms of means and ends and developing criteria for this purpose;

- introducing or developing shared training for women and men politicians, encouraging the sharing of experience not only between the sexes, but among both novices and seasoned veterans with respect to both failures and successes;

- ensuring that all policies for women's empowerment from inception onwards, include and target *men's* needs, fears, experiences and lessons learned;

- ensuring that the women who obtain positions of power and responsibility are provided with the tools necessary to enhance their political impact and are committed to the principles of gender equality as well as those of improving the status of women.

Some Concrete Suggestions for Good Governance Practices

An international "women and media" day can be used as a first step towards raising awareness both within and outside the international media community as the needs and constraints of women politicians and media personnel. Such an event should be sponsored by an international body and could include cyber-sessions and videoconferences with prominent and lay people from around the world. It could also lay the groundwork for a series of regional and/or local workshops to bring the two networks together.

Developing criteria for impacting as making a qualitative difference: Although "difference"

---

[44] Personal interview with BBC reporter, October 1998.
[45] Quotas have in some countries been imposed to increase the number of men in certain professions such as nursing and teaching.

is debatable because it is frequently subjective, women at all socio-cultural and economic levels have experiences that differ from those of men and that are reflected in different approaches, needs, insights and, often, goals. In her report, *Public Life: Women Make a Difference*, Virginia Willis argues that "the new political movement, the Greens, where women have from the beginning played a leading role, has tried new forms of politics and collaborative, non-hierarchical systems which also better reflect women's ways of working."[46] Similarly, in Sweden, Boman reports on a local council of a suburb which shows how an increase in women's representation to 40-48 per cent led to changes in the political climate with male officials acknowledging and prioritizing family obligations to broaden the context of decision-making, as well as debates that were more concise and focused, conducted in more accessible, concrete language.[47]

There are many points of view on what constitutes an "impact". Policy-specific examples include the following:

■ in the USA: a surge in day-care facilities and battered women's refuges. In addition, a number of private sector companies have developed diversity programmes that include building women's leadership skills, mentoring, and family-friendly policies to facilitate the juggling of many roles that women occupy;

■ in Australia: help pages in any telephone book include sections on domestic violence referral services, abortion counseling and rape crisis centres;

■ in Norway: changes in the "politics of motherhood" where care and career policies concerned with child-care institutions, working hours, as well as maternity leave, have generated an interest among political parties to adopt these as issues with which votes can be gained.[48]

Once again however, with the exception of the South African case, there is a serious paucity of information on more methods of impacting, as well as similar examples from elsewhere in the world.

The question that should be kept in mind constantly is: **To what extent has this kind of change taken place—if at all?** Given current media biases, difficulties and obstacles may gain attention at the expense of consistent attempts to realise changes, often so subtle as to escape immediate notice. Among these biases are:

■ *change in perception* of women and men politicians, as well as in the expected division of labour between men and women in any society. How politicians are perceived often makes or breaks political careers.

■ *change in discourse,* such as shifts in emphasis in women's participation in areas traditionally seen as "men's affairs" or "hard politics" (defense, finance, foreign policy), in addition to redefining and prioritizing "soft" issues such as welfare, maternity leave and education.

■ *change in coverage,* notably in the writing of textbooks and history (the seed of many of the female stereotypes that discourage women from entering public life), as well as media content.

■ *change in day-to-day workings of political institutions,* including family-friendly timing and location of meetings, as well as the *de facto* exclusion of women from traditional male caucus spaces, such as bars and all-male clubs.

Perhaps the most important lesson of Beijing, however, is the need to stop mythologising women's political capacities. The idea that a world governed equally by women and men will not necessarily be one of greater justice or less violence. The association of women with the "safe" "peaceful" or "equitable" haven of the home is fundamentally a cultural assumption. However persistent and pervasive world-wide, it is—like all cultural assumptions—subject to change. Further, no previous era has been marked by change as rapid as ours in virtually every domain. This pace is unlikely to slow. Finally, the myth of women as guardians of the home has been exploded by research on household inequities and domestic violence world-wide, as well as used to deter women from entering public space.

What we do know at the moment is that men and women have much to learn from one another in politics. However rapid that learning process may become and however much we need to take action

[46] See Virginia Willis, 1991. *Public Life: Women Make a Difference.* United Nations. V.91-24691. p. 10.
[47] Boman, Ann. 1987. *Every Other Slot to the Ladies.* Final Report from the Secretary of Labour's Project on Women's Representation. Stockholm.
[48] See also Hege Skjeie's case study on Norway "Credo on Difference" in Azza Karam, ed., *Women in Parliaments: Beyond Numbers,* pp. 183-190.

for its acceleration, the lessons require a great deal of internalization in addition to conscious mastery. The process is therefore likely to take longer than the acquisition of factual knowledge. Consequently, in assessing progress since Beijing, it is probably a good thing to bear in mind a Chinese proverb:

The [wo]man who built a mountain began by collecting small stones.

BIBLIOGRAPHY

Balch, Jeff, T. Bare and F. Gardiner (1998). *Achieving the Advancement of Women in the Post-Beijing Era.* Cape Town and Amsterdam: AWEPA/ African-European Institute.

Brill, Alida Ed. (1995). *A Rising Public Voice: Women in Politics Worldwide.* New York: The Feminist Press.

Bukley, Mary and M. Andersson, eds. (1988). *Women, Equality and Europe.* London: Macmillan.

Inter-Parliamentary Union. (1997a). *Towards Partnership between Men and Women in Politics: New Delhi (14-18 February).* Series Reports and Documents No. 29. Geneva: Inter-Parliamentary Union.

_____(1997b). *Men and Women in Politics: Democracy Still in the Making, A WorldComparative Study.* Series Reports and Documents No.28. Geneva: Inter-Parliamentary Union.

International Union of Local Authorities. (1998). *Women in Local Government.* Stockholm: IULA.

Karam, Azza, ed. (1998). *International IDEA Handbook on Women in Parliaments: Beyond Numbers.* Stockholm: International IDEA.

Karl, Marilee (1995). *Women and Empowerment: Participation and Decision-Making.* London and New Jersey: Zed Books.

Lovenduski, Joni (1986). *Women and European Politics: Contemporary Feminism and Public Policy.* Amherst, MA: University of Massachusetts Press.

Matland, Richard (1998). "Enhancing Women's Political Participation: Legislative Recruitment and Electoral Systems", in Azza Karam. Ed. 1998. *Women in Parliament: Beyond Numbers.* pp. 65-90.

Nelson, Barbara J. and N. Chowdhury, eds. (1994). *Women and Politics Worldwide,* New Haven and London: Yale University Press.

Netherlands Ministry of Foreign Affairs (1998). "Gender and Good Governance". Conference held in Harare, Zimbabwe (May). The Hague.

Norris, Pippa, ed. (1997). *Women, Media, and Politics.* New York, USA: Oxford University Press.

Phillips, Anne (1991). *Engendering Democracy.* Pennsylvania: Pennsylvania University Press.

Randall, Vicky (1987). *Women and Politics: An International Perspectives.* London: Macmillan.

Rule, Wilma and J. F. Zimmerman, eds. (1994). *Electoral Systems in Comparative Perspective: Their Impact on Women and Minorities.* Westport: Greenwood Press.

Staudt, Kathleen (1989). *"Women in High-Level Political Decision-making: A Global Analysis".* Vienna: United Nations Office, Division for the Advancement of Women.

United Nations Centre for Social Development and Humanitarian Affairs. (1992). *Women in Politics and Decision-Making in the Late Twentieth Century: A United Nations Study,* Dordrecht: Martinus Nijhoff Publishers.

UNDP. (1997). *Governance and Sustainable Growth and Equity: Report of International Conference.* New York.

_____ (1995). *Human Development Report.* New York.

UNDPI. (1995). *Platform for Action and the Beijing Declaration.* New York: United Nations Department of Public Information.

UNESCO. (1993). *Women in Politics: Australia, India, Malaysia, Philippines, and Thailand.* (Guest Editor: Latika Padgaonkar). Bangkok.

van der Ros, Janneke (1989). *Women in Politics: Does it Make a Difference? Women's Impact on the Public Agenda.* Annotated bibliography of literature from the USA and Nordic Countries, 1986-1989.

Willis, Virginia (1991). *Public Life: Women Make a Difference:* Expert group Meeting on the Role of Women in Public Life (Vienna, 21-24 May). New York: Division for the Advancement of Women.

WOMEN'S
POLITICAL
PARTICIPATION
AND GOOD
GOVERNANCE:
21ST CENTURY
CHALLENGES

26

GENDER, GOVERNANCE AND THE FEMINISATION OF POVERTY

SALLY BADEN[49]

What is the "feminisation of poverty" that has taken so significant a place in so much debate about the status of women? Will "good governance" in itself serve to reduce it? Similarly, will poverty reduction necessarily serve the advancement of gender equality? Why ask these questions at all?

Promoting choice and participation for women as well as for men has become increasingly pronounced in the general governance agenda—with, however, a tendency to assume that promoting participation for women and men revolves around the same mechanisms and that it will automatically promote women's interests. This assumption precludes recognising the gendered nature of institutions themselves (Ashworth, 1996).

This paper examines the links between gender, governance and poverty, highlighting the importance of institutional rules, norms and practices in determining entitlements and the ways in which they operate within families and underpin wider social phenomena.

Gender and Poverty

Conventional approaches to poverty definition and measurement based on income- consumption measures have been widely criticised for failing to capture human development outcomes (Sen, 1983; 1990; UNDP, 1997a). The use of the household as the unit of analysis in poverty measurement has also been the subject of much criticism from gender analysts. It is perfectly possible for women to be deprived in rich households and also for increases in household income to result in greater gender inequality in well-being (Kabeer, 1996; Jackson, 1996). According to Kabeer (1996; 1997), gender inequality and poverty result from distinct, interlocking, social relations and processes. This implies that the social relations of gender may act to exacerbate or relieve poverty for women in one context or another.

Given the unreliability of household income-based measures as a guide to the well-being of both women and men, poverty should be studied in terms of ends as well as means. A broader understanding, rooted in Sen's entitlements and

WOMEN'S POLITICAL PARTICIPATION AND GOOD GOVERNANCE: 21ST CENTURY CHALLENGES

---

[49] Sally Baden is the Manager of Bridge (Briefings on Development and Gender) and Lecturer at the Institute of Development Studies, University of Sussex, Brighton, the United Kingdom.

capabilities framework (1990b), has led to the development of a specific indicator—the Human Poverty Index or HPI—to monitor and compare experiences of human poverty over time (UNDP, 1997a; 1998). The HPI, alongside the HDI (Human Development Index) and GDI (Gender Development Index), provides the basis for comparing gendered experiences of well-being and deprivation, including those within the household (Cagatay, 1998).

However, although the HPI allows us to capture the magnitude of differences in actual well-being between men and women, it implicitly assumes those men and women experience deprivation in the same ways and face the same trade-offs. Yet lack of access to water, to take only one example, has different implications for both genders. Further, for women in a violent home, the trade-off between income and personal well-being is one that men do not face. A truly gendered understanding of well-being requires looking at additional factors, particularly issues of time use or experiences of violence that the HPI does not capture.

Gender analysts have developed Sen's framework to focus on the institutional rules, norms and practices from which entitlements are derived and specifically the gender biases that these embody (Kabeer, 1996). The range of entitlements that women can draw on may be circumscribed by rules, norms and practices that limit their market engagement. These include legal or other restrictions on occupations in which women may work, prevailing ideas about appropriate gender divisions of labour, or husbands' prohibitions on wives' working. Women may also have lesser endowments due to biases in feeding practices, unequal educational investments, or inheritance patterns. And the endowments they do have often yield lower returns because of gender segregation in the labour market or wage discrimination.

We can safely say that the gender bias in institutions that leads to differential entitlements and capabilities is characterised by:
(a) more constrained and weaker entitlements;
(b) more frequent entitlement failure;
(c) lower returns from translating entitlements and endowments into capabilities;
(d) a lesser degree of choice in determining capabilities.

The institutional rules, norms and practices governing households have great significance in reproducing gender differentials in entitlements and endowments. Women's engagement in paid labour, for example, is constrained by their care responsibilities in the home—while women's domestic work frees men to engage in market production.

Institutional rules, norms and practices are not externally imposed, immovable constraints. They are resources that are constantly drawn on and reconstituted in a variety of organisational settings. Women's exclusion from patriarchal decision-making structures, itself due to institutional biases, in turn, limits their capacity to influence rules, norms and practices that would bring about more gender-equitable policies and practices (Kabeer and Murthy, 1996).

Feminisation of Poverty

Are women poorer than men? The idea of a "feminisation of poverty" influenced the targeting of subsidies or micro-credit for women. But, as Cagatay (1998) points out, it has been used to mean three distinct things:

■ women have a higher *incidence* of poverty then men;

■ women's poverty is more *severe* that than of men;

■ there is a *trend* to greater poverty among women, particularly associated with rising rates of female headship of household.[50]

The evidence for a feminisation of poverty rests heavily on the rising incidence of female-headship of households[51] and the allied suggestion that such households are generally less well-off than their male-headed counterparts. But there are dangers in assuming that female headship always represents disadvantage. In cases where women choose to lead households, connotations of powerlessness and victimhood are inappropriate (Chant, 1997). Moreover, in female-headed households, women often have greater autonomy and control over resources. Well-being outcomes for women and children in these households may therefore be better than in male-headed households at the same level

WOMEN'S POLITICAL PARTICIPATION AND GOOD GOVERNANCE: 21ST CENTURY CHALLENGES

[50] Using income poverty as a criterion, the feminisation of poverty idea is hard to substantiate. Cagatay (1998) argues that if indicators of well-being associated with human poverty such as illiteracy are used, women, on average, are unambiguously worse off than men in almost all contexts.

[51] Data is patchy on the actual trends related to female headship and subject to wide variations in definition. There is some evidence of increased female headship in some countries (see e.g. Buvinic and Gupta, 1997).

of income (Kennedy and Peters, 1992; Kennedy and Haddad, 1994).

Responding to women's poverty must take account of the underlying institutional "rules of the game" (Goetz, 1995; Fraser, 1989, cited in Jackson, 1997). Where women are targeted with resources, it is often assumed that welfare benefits accrue directly to them and also to their children to a greater extent than resources targeted at men (Buvinic and Gupta, 1997). It has also been argued that where women gain access to external resources, perceptions of their value to the household may change, increasing their bargaining power, and leading to more equitable allocation of resources and decision-making power within the household (Sen, 1990a). Beyond this, claims have been made, for example, that credit programmes empower women economically, socially and politically, as well as in the context of the family (Hashemi *et al*, 1996).

But it is important to consider how power embedded in gender relations can modify these desired outcomes. Resources targeted to women may, for example, be siphoned off by men (Goetz and Sen Gupta, 1996). Men reduce their levels of contribution to household expenditure as women's access to resources increases (Bruce, 1989). Even where women do gain greater access to resources, this may increase their burden of labour, leaving them exhausted. Where they have control over resources, they may be unable to effectively mobilise these resources to support sustainable livelihoods. Women may feel compelled to invest resources, including their labour, in "family'" businesses, or in children, identifying their own interests with those of other household members, and thereby leaving themselves vulnerable in the event of family breakdown.

All these issues, along with others, point to the limitations of traditional micro-credit programmes in addressing women's poverty. Consequently, in the UNDP South Asian Poverty Alleviation Programme (SAPAP)—in which village development organisations form the basis for the savings and the allocation of loans by the organisations themselves—there is also investment in women's leadership and management skills (UNDP, 1998).

Governance and Poverty Reduction

The governance debate in development policy took off in the early 1990s,[52] with different influences

and interpretations of the issues (Moore, 1993). Narrow definitions of governance centre on economic and administrative governance (i.e. providing an enabling environment for private sector activity and reform of public administration); broader definitions encompass political governance, including the promotion of democratic political structures and human rights. In UNDP's definition, governance is *'the exercise of economic, political and administrative authority to manage a country's affairs at all levels. It comprises the mechanisms processes and institutions through which citizens and groups articulate their interests, exercise their legal rights, meet their obligations and mediate their differences.'* (UNDP, 1997a).

The increasing convergence of the governance and poverty reduction agendas stems in part from rethinking the nature of well-being and also from a broadening interpretation of governance to encompass political accountability and popular participation. Thus, to the extent that improved governance structures and processes lead to greater participation of the poor, this is assumed to improve their well-being.

Bilateral agency members of the OECD-DAC (Organisation for Economic Co-operation and Development Assistance Committee) have made more explicit linkages between political and economic objectives and made more direct claims for the developmental potential of political reform (DAC, 1994, cited in Goetz and O'Brien 1995). In recent UNDP literature, governance is increasingly stated as one of, if not the, key means to effective poverty reduction. Further, sustainable human development is posed as the goal of governance (UNDP, 1997b; UNDP, 1998). Rights-based approaches to poverty reduction have been adopted by some development agencies, like that of the United Kingdom (DFID, 1997). Similarly, according to UNDP, "Poverty needs to be redefined so as to include access to decision-making by both women and men and information on human rights" (UNDP, 1997c: 104). Current UNDP approaches to poverty reduction also stress the importance of empowerment as a means to address poverty, including that of women (UNDP, 1998).[53]

In linking the promotion of governance to poverty reduction, policy makers have tended to overem-

---

[52] Its popularisation is associated with the World Bank (1989) report *From Crisis to Sustainable Growth in Sub-Saharan Africa: A Long-Term Perspective Study.*

[53] The issue of empowerment as a means to poverty reduction, which is related to the governance approach, will not be addressed extensively in this report due to limitations of time and space.

phasise participation as an aspect of accountability, rather than of effectiveness and impact. It is often unclear how the participation of the poor is expected to lead to the articulation of their interests in ways which can influence institutional rules and practices (effectiveness), and consequently to different decisions about resource use that lead to poverty reduction in a material sense (impact).[54]

Typically, gender perspectives in the mainstream governance literature are limited to an examination of the need for more women in formal political life and strategies to achieve this, without consideration of the need for transformation of the institutions of power. This weakness becomes particularly important when focusing on the links between improved governance and the gendered causes and consequences of women's poverty. Here, numbers alone may be necessary, but are certainly not a sufficient condition, either for the articulation of (poor) women's gender interests or for their achieving an impact on resource allocation decisions and processes.

Although governance is about "getting institutions right for development" governance policies rarely concentrate on "getting institutions right for women in development" (Goetz, 1995). Outside the family, where the gendering of roles and behaviours is explicit but often assumed to be "natural", there is a tendency to assume that institutions[55] are neutral with respect to gender. Governance debates are no exception to this (Ashworth, 1996). However, "Familial norms and values are constantly drawn on in constructing the terms under which women and men enter and participate in public life and the market place" (Kabeer, 1996: 63). The public-private split that institutionalised women's exclusion from the public sphere and is also drawn on to reinforce gendered power relations in the public sphere. For example, women are confined to "typically" female tasks closely associated with their domestic roles, or more insidiously, subjected to sexual harassment or violence which both symbolically and literally threaten and contains women's identity as public actors (Goetz 1995).

Men's physical and historical dominance of the public sphere has meant that their needs and interests have become embedded in public institutions. Men's physical monopoly of public space means that everyday work patterns come to be structured around men's needs and capabilities, resulting in a gendered structuring of time and space in organisations. Ideologies and disciplines are also important in creating cognitive and cultural contexts that favour male interests. This is not immutable *(ibid.)*. However, confining reform efforts to measures to increase female representation in public life will have limited impact unless the broader constraints on women's meaningful participation are also addressed. It is important to recognise the interlocking forms of institutional exclusion faced by women, particularly poor women (Kabeer and Murthy, 1996). This implies a need to rethink and extend the scope of the current governance debate, and of related interventions, in order to increase "gender accountability".

Gender Accountability Across Institutional Contexts: Participation, Effectiveness and Impact

The practical limitations on women's **participation** in public and political debate are widely discussed in the development literature and elsewhere. The practical measures that may be necessary to include women in discussions and activities are well known (childcare provision, separate meetings where appropriate, consideration of women's workload and use of appropriate times and venues, language considerations) though less often actually implemented and adequately resourced. For poor women, these barriers are likely to be even greater.

Less discussed are the limitations on women's "voice". These relate to actual or perceived male resistance and silencing, internalised oppression and the difficulty of articulating women's interests within the existing framework of public debate. For poor women, the sense of powerlessness and exclusion is a product not just of their gender subordination, but of interlocking forms of exclusion linked also to class and race.

Improvements in women's participation do not necessarily mean that they will be *effective* in articulating their gender interests in public space. Where women are present in only small numbers, they may be marginalised and find it difficult to promote group interests. Women's immediate

WOMEN'S
POLITICAL
PARTICIPATION
AND GOOD
GOVERNANCE:
21ST CENTURY
CHALLENGES

---

[54] Here, the approach of Linda Mayoux (1998) to examining gender accountability is heavily drawn on and will be explained in more detail in later sections.

[55] Institutions are the formal and informal rules and constraints which shape social perceptions of needs and roles, while organisations administer these rules and respond to needs. Institutions create the context for organisations to operate. Over time, the latter can have an impact on former.

preoccupations may also reflect practical concerns that flow from existing divisions of labour and power, rather than more strategic challenges to underlying power structures. For this reason alone, it may take time before women articulate their gender interests effectively in the most strategic forums.

Once individual women gain access to positions of relative power, the problem of their accountability to the grass roots or poor women whom they "represent" arises. There is a danger that women in positions of power will be co-opted, or allow their gender interests to be subsumed by class, caste or ethnic interests. This may be exacerbated by their "newness to the club"—creating feelings of being beholden to others for their position. There are also very real divisions between women; some women have more to gain from preserving the status quo since their (albeit limited) power rests on their standing in the hierarchy over other women.

Finally, as participation in and openness of public institutions increases, gender interests emerge alongside many other issues, among these, children's rights, consumer's rights, housing and pollution. So participation may lead to greater competition over resources and also greater scope for men to organise to resist women's efforts to promote their gender interests. On the other hand, it creates opportunities for building strategic alliances between different interest groups.[56]

Accountability must also be assessed in terms of *impact*, i.e. changes in actual outcomes that improve women's lives, particularly those of poor women. Even where women are effective in articulating their gender interests, it does not always result in change. Certain areas of policy and decision-making (especially finance and economics, where decisions on resources are central) have been particularly resistant to incursions with a feminist agenda, in part because of their technical nature. Women, especially when in small numbers, are easily sidelined into "women's issues" in the social sectors, and may themselves feel more comfortable in such positions.

In addition, "unholy alliances" and "unruly practices" may impede women's efforts. "Unholy alliances" is a familiar term that connotes otherwise uncomfortable bedfellows—as in the concerted efforts of the Vatican and Islamist groups at the International

Conference on Population and Development (Cairo, 1994) and in the preparatory meetings for the Fourth World Conference on Women to resist the adoption of the term "gender" in the Beijing Platform for Action (Baden and Goetz, 1997). "Unruly practices" refer to formal or informal decisions that subvert norms or established rules. For example, in Uganda, a proposed amendment to the land legislation drawn up by women's groups and accepted by Parliament in the course of its debate mysteriously disappeared from the text of the law released after its adoption (Goetz and Jenkins, 1998) Both forces often conspire with bureaucratic inertia and insufficient resources to conspire against women's impact. Because of entrenched gender biases, women working in state bureaucracies to promote gender interests find themselves in an ambivalent position working both "within and against" the state. Most importantly the public/private divide implicit in state institutions— in which meeting women's needs is often construed as conflicting with the privacy of the home—has proved a barrier to establishing more equitable practices (Goetz, 1998).

All in all, while the issue of representation in formal political structures and arenas of decision-making is critical for women, a number of difficulties remain, notably in three areas:
(a) sustaining gains in these areas;
(b) ensuring that formal representation actually translates into meaningful participation; and
(c) ensuring that participation translates into substantive change in policies or decisions for resource allocation, which requires that gender interests become institutionalised. While liberal political democracy may create spaces for discussion of gender concerns, it does not automatically ensure better representation of women or their interests.

Legal Frameworks and Systems

Internationally and nationally, the establishment and popularisation of human rights instruments and legal provisions which provide for equality as well as protection from abuse, have drawn attention to the extent of gender-based disadvantage and discrimination. In particular, the recognition of violence against women as a human rights violation has been a breakthrough and has stimulated efforts to address gender violence in development policy and programmes. One notable example (to which a chapter of this collection is devoted) is the recent

---

[56] Whether gender, or class, mobilisation is seen as politically threatening in different contexts will differ (thanks to Nilufer Cagatay for this point).

United Nations interagency campaign to combat domestic violence against women in Latin America and the Caribbean.

However, the weakness of state interventions in promoting gender equality is widely acknowledged in the governance literature, and is attributed to the persistence of "customs and traditions [which] often undermine rules and regulations" (UNDP, 997c: 7). Legal measures on their own are insufficient and need to be accompanied by efforts to change values through education, training and media, as well as affirmative action to promote women's representation in politics and also the legal system *(ibid.)*.

Moreover, the frequent failure of legislative reform to uphold women's gender interests at local level is not just an issue of outmoded cultural values. Religious, traditional and judicial authorities administering personal or customary law can bring considerable influence to bear on political processes locally and nationally such that constitutional or formal legal provisions for gender equality can be undermined. In South Africa, for example, even with a progressive Constitution including extensive commitments to gender equality, the political need to accommodate traditional authorities as part of the post-apartheid settlement has militated against strong action to challenge these institutions over gender questions (Walker, 1994). The recent Magaya vs. Magaya case is another example, from Zimbabwe, where the provisions of the Legal Age of Majority Act (1982) were overruled in favour of customary law, which favours male inheritance (Thoko Rudvidzo, personal communication).

The failure of legal changes, even when accepted, to translate into meaningful change for poor women is also a result of their lack of capacity in the legal system. This results not only from women's lack of resources to access legal help, but from male dominance in the judicial system and from the social distance between poor women and legal systems, related to education and language. In cases involving domestic violence or sexual assault, unsympathetic or even abusive police responses, and fear of social ostracism, are added deterrents.

Macroeconomic Reform

The lack of consideration in macroeconomic policy of women's unpaid labour in the care economy has been described as a deeply embedded form of gender bias in macroeconomics (Elson, 1995a). This "gender bias", combined with the lack of technical skills among women in politics in economic analysis, has limited the impact of gender concerns on macroeconomic policy processes. Greater efforts are now made to assess the likely social and gender impacts of economic policies, but there is still a tendency to see the solution in terms of improving market access of the poor, with little consideration of the gender-specific barriers that women face in market engagement. The case for promoting labour-intensive growth in order to promote opportunities for the poor, for example, is gender biased in overlooking the fact that poor women, especially in rural areas, are rarely under-employed. It is the productivity of and returns to women's labour, inside as well as outside the household, that calls for improvement—not just their opportunities for further work.

Flowing from the lack of gender analysis in economic policy is a failure to analyse the likely impacts on poor women of changes in public expenditure, a key component of economic reform. Recent emphasis by the World Bank and other agencies on the protection of social expenditures and their reallocation to basic services holds potential benefits for poor women. But it is unclear to what extent these gains have actually been realised in the face of downward pressures on total budgets and the collapse of free public service delivery in many countries. Much wider use of the tools for impact analysis of public expenditure,[57] as well as more public scrutiny and debate over budgets *ex ante* as well as *ex post*, are needed in order to have a major impact here.

Recent initiatives from women in civil society, often working alongside women in government and with support from multilateral institutions, are beginning to make inroads into the domain of macroeconomic policy. In particular, the Women's Budget Initiative (WBI) in South Africa, learning from similar experiences in Australia (Budlender, 1998) has provided inspiration for the establishment of similar initiatives in a number of other countries, particularly in the Southern African region. South Africa is now also one of three pilot countries for a broader initiative to engender macroeconomic policy, formally under the aegis of government.

---

[57] For example, the tools of gender-disaggregated benefit incidence analysis.

These initiatives are simultaneously addressing the issue of engaging women in economic policy debates, changing the rules and practices—through efforts to reform the budgetary process—and ensuring that actual resource allocation decisions take account of women's interests. Most importantly, perhaps, they are pushing for policies that give intrinsic value to human life, as well as adequate recognition of women's labour in producing and sustaining human life.

Other initiatives to monitor and influence the impact of macroeconomic regulatory frameworks on poor women include the work of the Council for the Economic Empowerment of Women in Africa (CEEWA) in Uganda. CEEWA have lobbied for changes to economic legislation (the recent Financial Institutions Act 1993 and Bank of Uganda Statute 1993) enacted in the context of financial sector reform. These efforts are intended to ensure that such legislation does not institutionalise discrimination or biases against poor women who are the main beneficiaries of non-formal micro-enterprise finance (Kiggundu, 1998). Networks of grassroots women's organisations in the informal sector have also been effective in influencing policy at both national and international levels leading to the adoption of the ILO Convention on Homeworking (Tate, 1996; Prugl and Tinker, 1997).

Public Sector Restructuring and Service Provision

Although no longer seen as providers of universally free services, or as having a monopoly on service delivery, governments are still widely held to have a central role as providers of a safety net for the poor and vulnerable. This includes providing an appropriate policy and institutional framework for poverty reduction efforts, collecting and using public revenues in ways which maximise their poverty impact and, increasingly, designing policies and delivering services in ways that empower the poor, or give them "voice".

Reform of the public administration is a key element of governance strategies. It encompasses a wide range of measures, including downsizing and restructuring the civil service, introducing new human resources policies and management systems, and efforts to end or reduce corruption. Reform of the public sector often involves introducing competition into service delivery and contracting

out service provision to voluntary sector or private providers, or service provision in partnership with non-government actors. While this can improve the quality of service provision and outreach to poorer groups, it has disadvantages from an accountability perspective.

Where a whole range of service providers are operating at a small-scale, localised level, it is hard to have a co-ordinated approach, particularly on strategic issues such as gender policy. A proliferation of service providers may also prove difficult to hold accountable, since there is no clear focus for complaint or lobbying and public administrations may find compliance hard to enforce. Where front-line personnel in service provision organisations (often women) have poor conditions of pay and work of, this can have very negative consequences on access to and quality of services available, due to absenteeism, de-motivation and *de facto* 'privatisation'.[58]

Research on the experiences of poor people has highlighted the problem of social distance between poor people (especially women users of social services) and providers or administrators of public services. This reinforces experiences of exclusion and powerlessness faced by many poor people. The disrespect of service providers towards the culture and views of poor clients sometimes encompasses verbal and even physical abuse and harassment, as in documented cases of nurses beating patients. Women and girls may be particularly susceptible to abuse and harassment of various kinds, such as sexual harassment of girls by male schoolteachers.

National Machineries

The main instrument through which support for women's gender interests has been mobilised within government structures to date is national machineries for women. These have made many positive achievements, most importantly legitimising the place of gender issues in development planning (Goetz, 1998). However, these mechanisms suffer from a history of marginalisation and insecurity, under-resourcing, lack of technical capacity, over-reliance on donor funding and, in some cases, lack of accountability to constituencies in civil society. The fact that many national machineries have been established during periods of fiscal restraint and

---

[58] Whereby fees are charged for services which are nominally free, in order to supplement low incomes of public sector workers.

government restructuring has made their claims on resources difficult to advance (Byrne *et al*, 1995). In other words, there are serious questions about effectiveness and impact.

Some lessons have been learned. National machineries set up following democratic transitions (e.g. Philippines, Chile, South Africa, Uganda) have been relatively influential and effective because of the context of broad commitment to greater social equality and justice. Positive experiences also highlight the importance of broad and open processes of consultation, for example, in the development of national gender policies.

Latterly, mainstreaming strategies have become the focus of efforts to institutionalise gender in state bureaucracies. These are reaching beyond traditionally "female" arenas into "hard" ministries such as finance, planning and agriculture—which, in turn, has highlighted a lack of technical skills among gender advocates, as well as the need for heightened awareness of gender issues among technical staff in line ministries, where implementation responsibility should remain.

It is also unclear to what extent national machineries have prioritised the needs and interests of *poor women*. Given limited resources, this is critical. Certainly, there are positive examples: the *Servicio Nacional de la Mujer* (SERNAM) in Chile launched a major programme targeting poor female headed households in 1994/5; in South Africa, poor, African, rural women are a major stated focus of the Commission on Gender Equality, the statutory body charged with monitoring government and other actions to promote gender equality.

Decentralisation

Participation of the poor in the decentralised management of service delivery has been a major plank of governance efforts on the assumption that this will make service provision more accountable and response to the interests of the poor. Unlike central government, local authorities and agencies are perceived to be closer to the people and more directly accountable. But this assumption overlooks the possibility that at the local level, power elites may be more entrenched than at the national and more hostile to demands from marginalised groups (Griffin, cited in Goetz and O'Brien, 1995; UNDP, 1998).

Implicit in some of the governance literature is the idea that decentralisation is inherently favourable to women because it reduces logistical and other barriers to their participation and will lead to greater responsiveness of locally provided services to the needs of women as major users of these services. Recent moves to increase participation in local planning processes—such as the Law of Popular Participation in Bolivia, introduced in conjunction with decentralisation—are also seen as offering opportunities for the direct participation of women, among others, to influence the design of services to meet their needs.

However, women do not necessarily achieve greater representation at the local level as compared to national. There are both positive and negative examples here. In India, decentralisation has been used as a vehicle for promoting women's representation with a requirement to reserve one third of seats for women in local government, thus resulting in a huge increase in the numbers of women active in political life.[59] Elsewhere, democratic transitions and national quotas adopted by political parties have ensured high levels of representation of women in Parliament, but this has not always been reflected at the local level, South Africa is a case in point. While women hold 27 per cent of the South African Parliamentary seats, they attained only 19 per cent of representation in local government elections (Budlender and de Bruyn, 1998). Outside formal local politics, women are often very involved in community action, but this can remain invisible because of its informal nature. Even where new participatory structures are put in place, which might enable more access for informal women's associations, other political imperatives, such as the ethnic politics of indigenous representation, may take precedence over gender interests (Lind, 1997).

Decentralisation of service delivery (e.g. of health services), when combined with an emphasis on increased cost-recovery, can also result in reduced access for the poor, reduced capacity for cross-subsidisation between services and localities and thus increased inequalities in service provision (Baden, 1992). Where the management of school provision has been decentralised or contracted out to the private sector, there is evidence of middle class capture and dominance leading to increased fees in good schools and thus the exclusion of children from poorer households (Turner and Hulme, 1997; Goetz and O'Brien, 1995).

---

[59] This experience is analysed in one of the other conference background papers.

Thus the responsiveness of decentralised services to women's needs appears to depend on available resources and competition over these, on the nature of local power structures, and on the degree of organisation and political visibility of women locally. Intergovernmental fiscal relations can be designed such that equity concerns are given a weighting in the allocation of resources from central to local government, but these tend to focus on interregional disparities. There may be instances where this benefits women for demographic reasons (e.g. where women predominate in poorer rural areas) but this is a blunt instrument (Budlender and De Bruyn, 1998). Where women are required to represent their interests at many different levels, this increases the difficulty of articulating aggregated interests that might have a major policy impact.

Markets and the Private Sector

Discussions of governance tend to focus more on the structures and processes related to public administration than on the market. This is perhaps consonant with the role of "good government" in underpinning market liberalisation in the context of macroeconomic adjustment. Discussions of market governance are thus relatively less developed in relation to the interests of the poor and other marginalised groups.[60]

Nonetheless, feminist economists have analysed the embeddedness of markets in gendered institutions (Harriss-White, 1998) and the ways in which markets act as bearers of gender (Elson, 1995b) in relation not only to labour, but also financial and product markets (Baden, 1998a, 1998b). This reflects the social and spatial organisation of markets, in which women tend to be confined to individuated enterprises and restricted to certain points in the marketing chain or geographical spheres of operation. It also reflects gender ideology, whereby certain goods or skills are deemed to be "female" and therefore "inferior" (Harris-White, op cit.). Women's relative lack of access to formal financial services and their related reliance on informal sector finance can be understood in terms of gendered transaction costs in credit markets, linked to regulatory frameworks and institutional norms

(Baden, 1998a). From this perspective, measures to increase women's activity in micro-enterprise, for example, while leaving unaddressed the institutional rules and norms governing the financial system,[61] will tend to replicate existing patterns of gender segmentation in markets. These confine the majority of women entrepreneurs and "family workers" to the low-profit, high competition informal sphere, where prospects for accumulation are weak.

Different approaches have been attempted to institutionalise more gender-equitable market governance. At international level, the development of codes of conduct governing trade relationships between northern corporations and southern producers arc one mechanism being explored from a gender perspective (Fontana et al, 1998). The extension of labour legislation to offer protection to workers in sectors or occupational categories where poor women are concentrated, e.g. domestic work, casual agricultural labour, informal sector trading or homeworking, providing it is backed by effective monitoring and enforcement procedures, is one way to reduce gender-discriminatory practices. Support to the development of organisations of informal sector workers/ street traders and other low-paid workers who lack representation and protection is another, through action research and promoting dialogue with authorities, employers and formal sector trade unions over key issues. Through organisations such as the South African Women's Union and the Working Women's Forum and the Self-Employed Women's Association in India, services can also be provided to unprotected workers, such as basic health care and insurance, or legal aid (Tate, 1996).

Civil Society

"Civil society" encompasses the range of voluntary associations in between the family and the state. It is seen as important in providing check and balances on the actions of the state and the private sector, in empowering the poor, and ensuring their effective participation in safety nets and other poverty reduction programmes. It has a key role in responding to state and market "failure" through voluntary provision of various kinds, and more generally in reducing the transactions costs of

GENDER, GOVERNANCE AND THE FEMINISATION OF POVERTY

---

[60] The internal procedures and structures of private sector organisations has also started to come under scrutiny with the development of social auditing methodologies although the extent to which gender concerns are incorporated into these is not clear.

[61] This financial system has many elements, e.g. the organisational procedures and culture of banks; segregation of the financial system into formal and informal segments; the ways in which different financial instruments and securities are defined.

economic and social development (UNDP, 1997d; Robinson, 1995).

A general problem with analyses of civil society in the governance literature is that is tends to be portrayed as virtuous, non-conflictual and functional in social development. Clearly, however, there are strong conflicts between interest groups (including gender-based interest groups; or groups with strongly opposed gender ideologies) in civil society, such that promoting civil society will not necessarily result in outcomes that increase gender accountability. Examples include welfare organisations linked to conservative religious groups or other groups that may have widespread networks of social provision (health care, schooling etc.) involving poor people, but that exclude girls and women, or relegate them to narrowly gendered roles.

There are a number of ways in which the constitution of civil society reflects gendered norms and practices. The spaces for women to mobilize in civil society may be relatively restricted, such that they belong to a narrow range of organisations that are gender-typed, gender-segregated or less politically influential. For example, poor women tend to be dominant as members of religious groups rather than trade unions, political parties and business associations, which have a more direct line into policy processes. Where women are active, it tends to be in mobilizing support among women for organisational objectives, rather than organizing around gender interests. Even women's organisations do not necessarily provide space for the articulation of gender interests; they may in fact promote highly conservative agendas. Explicitly feminist groups are often characterised as elitist, urban-based and middle-class. There are divisions between organisations focused on lobbying and advocacy and those engaged in direct service provision, the latter sometimes involved in more immediate demands from poor women.

Poor women are engaging in a variety of forms of community action and creating alternative organisations and movements, not necessarily motivated primarily by feminist agendas, but in response to processes of economic, social and political exclusion (Lind, 1997). However, rarely do these fragmented forms of organisation result in the articulation of aggregated gender interests in political movements of a durable nature (Mayoux, 1988; Lind, 1997). The problem is that the organisational forms in which women mobilize is often not recognised in political systems. And

where networks or associations formed by women (e.g., around water use management; rotating credit associations) become formalized, positions of authority may be taken over by men.

In relation to poverty reduction objectives, the often presumed comparative advantage of NGOs and grassroots organisations in reaching the poor is not always based on rigorous analysis or evidence. Grassroots organisations and social movements may be genuinely participatory in their approach and some NGOs have been instrumental in developing and applying participatory methods of working with local communities. Nevertheless, there are many examples of NGOs dominated by charismatic leaders and run in an autocratic fashion (Turner and Hulme, 1997).

Equally, research to date suggests that in the absence of specific goals of promoting gender equity, there is no necessary correspondence between management democracy in organisations and institutional comparative advantage. Consequently, NGOs do not necessarily provide a more congenial environmental for the institutionalisation of women's interests than state bureaucracies. Promotion of NGOs, or even women's organisations, then, should not be seen as an automatic panacea for improving gender accountability.

There remain many differences between women at all these levels in terms of their interests and priorities, as well as appropriate strategies to advance these. But there is also considerable evidence of networks and alliances developing around strategic issues, which link women internationally, as well as across the "domains'" of civil society, private sector and state. (Miller and Razavi, 1998). There is much to be learned from the experiences of these networks and their attempts to hold international organisations accountable.

Family Governance: the Missing Link in Governance Debates

While governance and poverty debates have been primarily concerned with issues of government failure and to a lesser extent market failure, equally important from a gender perspective are policies that provide a response to "family failures", (Kabeer and Humphrey, 1991) in particular:

- the failure of many families to provide a safe or secure environment which promotes women's and children's well-being (e.g., in terms of adequate nutrition, rest and freedom from violence and abuse);

- men's reluctance to contribute to household and child maintenance financially and in terms of provision of care and domestic work;

- failure of institutional and welfare arrangements governing families to provide women with effective choice beyond exit.

According to UNDP, governance is described as "encompassing every institution and organisation in a society - from the family to the state" (1997d). However, to date, governance debates have paid little attention to issues of family governance,[62] which has remained in the domain of social policy.[63] As stated in the earlier analysis of gender and poverty, understanding the ways in which the rules, norms and practices within households underpin wider forms of bias is critical to addressing gendered poverty.

Conclusions and Key Recommendations

The current literature on governance tends to conflate goals, and assume positive links between governance and poverty reduction on the one hand and, on the other, between poverty reduction and gender disadvantage. The popular notion of the feminization of poverty, when interpreted as a universal phenomenon has contributed to analytical confusion and to policies which target female heads of household, or even more loosely, women, as a means to poverty reduction.

This report has highlighted the importance of recognising the gender-differentiated entitlements that lead to different experiences of poverty among men and women. In turn, these are determined by institutional rules, norms and practices that have differential outcomes. Consequently, a gender analysis of institutions is essential to understanding the links between gender, poverty and governance. In particular, in order to support governance processes that will impact on women's poverty, it is important that institutions improve their gender accountability. Institutional accountability with regard to women's gender interests is assessed here at the levels of participation, effectiveness and impact.

The lack of attention, in general, to issues of power and conflict in governance debates leads to a tendency to underplay differences of interests, including gender interests, between social groups and therefore to underestimate the level of *political* resistance to gender re-distributive change. Resource allocation decisions that favour the poor may engender negative reactions not just from men, but also from some women. This expresses itself not just in formal institutional structures and rules, but also through "unruly practices" that undermine formal rules and "unholy alliances" that form to resist changes.

Attempts to promote women's gender interests need to utilize governance and poverty agendas more effectively, at the levels of both discourse and intervention. This might include questioning and reinterpreting concepts (e.g., civil society) and their apparent gender neutrality, as well as broadening the debate to include discussions of gender equity related to family governance, which currently receive little attention. At the same time, development co-operation efforts must ensure that gender issues are not confined to particular spheres of governance. Crucially, the tendency within governance agendas to reinforce public/private divides must be critically re-examined.

Development co-operation efforts to support gendered governance for poverty reduction must also recognize the new forms of organizing, networking and alliance-building in which women are engaged—even though they may be transient and informal—as legitimate political actors. This requires a broadening of the definition of the political, and interventions that create spaces for women's organizing, as well as their alliance-building.

[62] Paradoxically, though, issues of "private" morality are being played out in public political arenas in unprecedented ways. Recent crises of governance relating to the perceived legitimacy of powerful individuals in public office (e.g. US and Malaysia) have centred on public exposure of "private" sexual behaviour. Male politicians are being held publicly accountable and vilified for transgressing idealised norms of familial loyalty and trust in unprecedented ways. In the past, such 'double standards' have been acceptable behaviour for men in public office. Thanks to Maila Stivens for this point. The case in Nicaragua, of Zoilamerica Narvaez and her accusation of sexual abuse against her stepfather Daniel Ortega, has thus far met with a very different response, however. Ortega has invoked his parliamentary immunity to evade answering charges in court.

[63] Indeed, the state has intervened in the "private" sphere of the family in highly gendered ways, e.g., in reproductive health programmes, social welfare programmes etc.

KEY RECOMMENDATIONS FOR DEVELOPMENT CO-OPERATION TO SUPPORT GENDER EQUITABLE GOVERNANCE FOR POVERTY REDUCTION

Critical assessments of experience in promoting good government through development co-operation signal a need for caution in this area. Political conditionalities attached to governance agenda, have, in the main, not proved useful (IDS, 1995). Supporting processes of institution building is inherently difficult. In promoting civil society, there is a danger of ideological bias, of distorting processes of institutional development, or of weakening accountability to domestic constituency while increasing accountability to external donors (Moore, 1993; Robinson, 1995).

The promotion of gender equality goals via institution-building in government and outside has been particularly susceptible to reliance on donor agencies and to accusations of cultural imperialism, particularly where gender ideology is highly contested. There is a danger of a negative backlash with implications for indigenous feminisms (Goetz, 1998). Donors need to be highly sensitive to the potentially counterproductive results of interventions in this area. The language and mechanisms employed in pursuing gender goals will be critical.

Below are some brief pointers to areas that require more attention in development co-operation. Broadly, poverty reduction requires greater focus on the effectiveness and impact aspects of gender account-ability, as well as its "participation" dimension.

Government

Economic Policy and the Budgetary Process

Continued efforts to institutionalize gender budgets in government and to revise macroeconomic models and policy frameworks to incorporate gender concerns are required. However it is equally important to maintain support for initiatives 'outside' government, and particularly to build links between feminist economic analysis and the grassroots mobilisation of women. More broadly, efforts to increase the transparency and accountability of budgetary processes should be driven by objectives of equity and participation, rather than fiscal restraint. In policy dialogue with governments, donors could give far greater prominence to poverty reduction and gender equity concerns. They could also set a much-improved example by redistributing their aid allocations to the social sectors and to specific items within these sectors.

Democratisation

Promoting women in political life at both the national and local levels requires attention to building links and dialogue between women inside and outside political structures to build accountability, particularly in periods of legislative change. Equally, support is required to develop the technical and political skills of women representatives to intervene in legislative processes. Beyond this, reform of electoral systems needs to take account of the impact of different voting systems in terms of women's participation and representation.

Legal Rights

A stronger focus is needed on economic and social rights and on their implementation, such as maintenance and land reform and titling.[64] Support mechanisms are needed for women to claim legal entitlements (awareness-raising, legal aid, resources for land registration etc.). Research on localized interpretations of customary or personal law may reveal possibilities for increasing women's choices. "Test cases" may be needed in conflicts between national/ constitutional and customary law over issues of gender equity. Legal aid provision needs to be made via organisations that directly engage poor women (e.g. informal sector unions) in areas related to their work and also to tackle individual problems experienced in their family or personal life.

National Machineries and Public Sector Services

Women working within the state to promote women's interests need to cultivate relationships with external constituencies more actively, even where these are perceived as critical and hostile. Such women should also exploit policy agendas

---

[64] Maintenance here is understood as payments to separated or divorced women normally from former partners (though in some instance payments from the state are referred to as maintenance grants) intended for the support of children and in some instances the woman herself.

on governance and poverty reduction more effectively (Goetz, 1998).

Efforts at public sector restructuring to improve service delivery should focus on the qualitative issues surrounding relations between clients and providers. Incentive systems in public sector management should be related to targets of equitable as well as efficient service delivery and improved impacts or outcomes for beneficiaries. There is a need to ensure that the restructuring of service provision has positive impacts in terms of employment and training opportunities for personnel in vital front-line provision roles, who are most likely to interact directly with women and children. This is important to ensure that staff are retained and motivated and that clients can choose providers of a specific gender where they prefer. Finally, punitive measures are required to address pervasive sexual harassment of both colleagues and clients in public sector organisations.

Decentralisation

There is a critical need to improve accountability systems and budgetary analysis skills at the local government level. Supporting local government federations to develop and promote improved practice with regard to gender analysis and planning aimed at poverty reduction may be an appropriate mechanism.

In terms of participation in local planning processes, it is critical to address poor women's perspectives in areas such as urban housing and infrastructure development. Two key areas here are the importance women attach to their homes as spheres of productive as well as "reproductive" activity and their needs for transport provision that responds to the many demands on women's lives. Conversely, municipal planning decisions and regulations need to ensure that women's informal sector activities are neither prevented nor displaced.

Private Sector

More basic research is needed on the gendered outcomes of market processes, drawing on the innovative analyses of feminist economists. Areas of possible intervention include the extension of labour legislation to cover unprotected workers (which must be matched by enforcement powers); support to the development of informal sector

unions and associations of casual workers in different sectors; and the creation of statutory bodies with oversight authority on gender equity issues in the private as well as public sectors. Support to the development and institutionalisation of gender auditing methods relevant to private sector organisations would also be valuable.

Civil Society

Mechanisms for support to civil society and NGOs need to include criteria related to strengthening or developing gender accountability. Support to civil society should also include encouragement to efforts at networking, association and federation of such entities as existing small-scale credit unions or informal sector unions, where low-income women are likely to be concentrated. More support should be channeled to NGOs active in lobbying and advocacy work on gender (from a pro-poor perspective), not just those engaged in service delivery with immediate impacts on poverty. This should include support for these organisations to engage in dialogue with government ministries, donors and others.

Lastly, there is a case for encouraging the development of grassroots organisations in areas or regions where gender disparities are particularly marked and social indicators poor. However, such efforts need to start from "where women are" and build support through long-term sustainable relationships, rather than short-term financial support.

Family Governance

Legislative and policy frameworks are required that promote choice and flexibility in family arrangements (e.g., facilitating female-initiated divorce), that recognize the wide variety of existing households and their fluid nature, and that grant equal or parallel status to different family types, irrespective of their perceived moral legitimacy. There should be stronger measures to prevent women from falling into poverty or destitution in the event of family breakdown or bereavement. At the same time, it should be remembered that family breakdown may leave single men highly vulnerable where they have limited networks of social support. Social provisioning linked to care (e.g. child benefits) should be paid to carers irrespective of gender.

BIBLIOGRAPHY

Ashworth, G. (1996). "Gendered governance: an agenda for change." *UNDP Gender Monograph Series* No. 3, UNDP, New York, March.

Baden, S. (1998a). "Gender issues in financial liberalisation and financial sector reform", *BRIDGE Report* No. 39. IDS, Brighton.

_____(1998b). "Gender issues in agricultural market liberalisation", *BRIDGE Report* No. 41, IDS, Brighton.

_____(1992). "Gender and adjustment in Sub-Saharan Africa", *BRIDGE Report*, IDS, Sussex.

Baden, S. and A. M. Goetz (1997). "Who needs [sex] when you can have [gender]: discourses on gender at Beijing" in *Feminist Review*, No. 57, Spring.

Baden, S., with K. Milward (1995). "Gender and poverty", *BRIDGE Report* No. 30, IDS, Sussex.

Beall, J., (1996). "Urban governance: why gender matters", *UNDP Gender Monograph Series* No. 1., UNDP, New York, March

Bruce, J. (1989). "Homes divided", *World Development*, 24 (3), the Netherlands.

Budlender, Debbie and J. De Bruyn (1998). "Intergovernmental fiscal relations", chapter 2 in Budlender, D (1998a) (Ed.) *The Third Women's Budget.* Idasa, Cape Town.

Budlender, D. (1998). "The South African Women's Budget Initiative", background paper no. 2 for the 'Meeting on Women and Political Participation: 21st Century Challenges, UNDP, 24-26 March, 1999, New Delhi, India

Buvinic and Gupta, G. R. (1997). "Female headed households and female-maintained families: are they worth targeting to reduce poverty in developing countries?", in *Economic Development and Cultural Change*, Vol. 45, No 2.

Byrne, B., J. Koch Laier, S. Baden and R. Marcus (1996). "National Machineries for Women in Development. Experiences lessons and strategies for institutionalizing gender in development policy and planning", *BRIDGE Report* No. 36, IDS, Brighton

Cagatay, N. (1998). "Gender and poverty" *UNDP Social Development and Poverty Elimination Division, Working Paper Series*, No. 5. May.

Chant, S. (1997). "Women-headed households: poorest of the poor? Perspectives from Mexico, Costa Rica and the Philippines", *IDS Bulletin*, Vol. 28, No. 3, IDS, Brighton

Department for International Development (DFID) (1997). *Eliminating World Poverty: A Challenge for the 21st Century*, UK Government White Paper on International Development, November

Elson, D. (1994). "Economic paradigms and their implications for models of development: the case of human development", contribution to Essays in honour of G.K. Helleiner, University of Manchester (draft, mimeo).

Elson, D. (1995a). "Male bias in macroeconomics: the case of structural adjustment", in Elson, D. (1995) (ed.). *Male Bias in the Development Process:* Manchester University Press, Contemporary Issues in Development Studies, Second Edition.

Elson, D. (1995b), "Rethinking strategies for development: from male-biased to human-centred development" in Elson, D., (ed.), 1995, *Male Bias in the Development Process*, Second Edition, Manchester University Press

Fontana, M., S. Joekes, and R. Masika (1998). "Global trade expansion and liberalisation: gender issues and impacts", *Briefings on Development and Gender (BRIDGE) Report* No 42, commissioned by the Department for International Development, UK, Institute of Development Studies, University of Sussex

Goetz, A .M. (1998). "Mainstreaming gender equity to national development planning", in Miller, C and Razavi, S (1998). (eds.) *Missionaries and Mandarins: Feminist Engagement with Development Institutions*, ITDG, London

Goetz, A. M. and R. Jenkins (1998). "Creating a framework for reducing poverty: institutional and process issues in national poverty policy: Uganda Country Report", Report to DFID (Draft), Institute of Development Studies, November 30

Goetz, A. M. and D. O'Brien (1995). "Governing for the common wealth? The World Bank's Approach to poverty and governance" in *IDS Bulletin*, Vol. 26, No. 2, April

Goetz, A. M. (1995). "Institutionalizing women's interests and gender-sensitive accountability in development", Editorial in "Getting institutions right for women in development" *IDS Bulletin*, Vol. 26 No 3, July

Goetz, Anne Marie and Rina Sen Gupta (1996). "Who takes the credit? Gender power and control over loan use in rural credit programs in Bangladesh'", *World Development*, 24 (1), The Netherlands

Harriss-White, B. (1998). "Female and male grain marketing systems: Analytical and policy issues for West Africa and India", in Jackson, C and Pearson, R (eds.) (1998). *Feminist Visions of Development: Gender Analysis and Policy*, Routledge, London

Hashemi, Syed, Schuler, Ruth Sidney and Ann Riley (1996). "Rural credit programs and women's empowerment in Bangladesh", *World Development*, 24 (4),

Healey, J., and W. Tordoff, (eds.) (1995). *Votes and Budgets: Comparative Studies In Accountable Governance in the South,* International Political Economy Series, Macmillan/ODI, London

IFAD (1992). *The State of the World Rural Poverty, An Inquiry into its Causes and Consequences*, by I. Jazairy and M. Alamgir, International Fund for Agricultural Development, Rome, Italy.

Institute of Development Studies (IDS) (1995). "Can aid promote good government?" *IDS Policy Briefing*, Issue 2, February, IDS, Brighton

Jackson, C (1996). "Rescuing gender from the poverty trap", *World Development*, Vol. 23 No. 4

Kabeer (1997). Editorial in "Tactics and trade-offs: the links between gender and poverty revisited", *IDS Bulletin* Vol. 28 No. 3, IDS, Brighton

Kabeer, N. (1996). "Agency, well-being and inequality" in *IDS Bulletin* Vol. 27 No. 1, IDS, Brighton.

Kabeer, N. and R. K. Murthy (1996). "Compensating for institutional exclusion? Lessons from Indian government and non-government credit interventions for the poor", *IDS Discussion Paper* No. 356, IDS, Brighton.

Kabeer, N., and J. Humphrey (1991). "Neoliberalism, gender and the limits of the market", in Colclough, C., and Manor, J., (1991). *States or Markets? Neoliberalism and the Development Policy Debate,* Clarendon Press, Oxford.

Karam, A., ed. (1998). *Women in Parliament: Beyond Numbers.* Handbook Series. International Institute for Democracy and Electoral Assistance, Stockholm.

Kennedy, E. and L. Haddad (1994). "Are pre-schoolers from female-headed households less malnourished? A comparative analysis of results from Ghana and Kenya", in *The Journal of Development Studies*, 30:3, 680-695.

Kennedy, E. and P. E. Peters (1992). "Household food security and child nutrition: the interaction of income and gender of household head", *Development Discussion Paper* no. 417, Harvard Institute for International Development, Cambridge: Harvard University.

Kiggundu, R. (1998). "Loosening the purse strings: financial sector reform in Uganda" in *Development and Gender In Brief*, No. 7, February, BRIDGE, IDS

Leftwich, Adrian (1994). "Governance, the state and the politics of development", *Development and Change*. Vol. 25, No 2., 363-386.

Lind, A. (1997). "Gender, development and urban social change: women's community action in global cities", *World Development*, Vol. 25, No 8

Mayoux, L. (1998). "Gender accountability and NGOs: avoiding the black hole", in Miller, C. and Razavi, S (1998) *Missionaries and Mandarins: Feminist Engagement with Development Institutions*, ITDG, London

Miller, C. and S. Razavi (1998). Introduction, in Miller, C and Razavi, S (1998). (eds.) *Missionaries and Mandarins: Feminist Engagement with Development Institutions*, ITDG, and London.

Moore, M. (1993). Introduction, in "Good government?" *IDS Bulletin*, Vol. 24, No 1, January

Prugl, E. and I. Tinker (1997). "Microentrepreneurs and homeworkers: convergent categories" *World Development*, 25 (9)

Quisumbing, A. R. et al (1995). "Gender and poverty: new evidence from 10 developing countries", International Food Policy Research Institute (IFPRI) *Food Consumption and Nutrition Division Discussion Paper* No. 9, IFPRI, Washington DC.

Robinson, M. (1995). Introduction in "Towards democratic governance", *IDS Bulletin* Vol. 26 No 2., April

Sen, A. (1990b). "Development as capability expansion", in Griffin, K and Knight, J. (1990). *Human Development and the International Development Strategy for the 1990s*, Macmillan, United Nations.

Sen, A. (1990a). "Gender and cooperative conflicts" in I. Tinker, (ed.), *Persistent Inequalities*, Clarendon, Oxford

Tate, J. (1996). "Making links: the growth of homeworker networks", in Boris, E and Prugl, E (Ed) (1996). *Homeworkers in Global Perspective: Invisible no More*, Routledge, London

Turner, M and Hulme, D (1997). *Governance, Administration and Development: Making the State Work*, Macmillan

UNDP (1995). *Human Development Report 1995*, UNDP, New York

UNDP (1997a). *Human Development Report 1997*, UNDP, New York

UNDP (1997b). "Governance for sustainable human development", UNDP Policy Paper Paper, UNDP, New York

UNDP (1997c). *Governance for Sustainable Growth and Equity: Report of an International Conference*, United Nations, New York, 28-30 July 1997

UNDP (1997d). "Reconceptualizing governance", *MAGNET Discussion Paper* No 2 UNDP, New York, January.

UNDP (1998). *Overcoming Human Poverty: UNDP Human Poverty Report, 1998*, UNDP, New York

Walker, C. (1994). "Women, 'tradition' and reconstruction", *Review of African Political Economy*, No. 61: 347-58.

CHAPTER 5

WOMEN IN THE PANCHAYATI RAJ: GRASSROOTS DEMOCRACY IN INDIA

POORNIMA VYASULU AND VINOD VYASULU[65]

The 1993-94 elections in India brought about some 800,000 women into active political life as a result of the 73rd and 74th amendments to the Constitution which promulgated that one third of the seats in local councils, both urban and rural—the gram Panchayats (GP)—be allotted to women. Moreover, the GPs were given the responsibility for designing, implementing and monitoring social services—notably health and education—and anti-poverty programmes.

Traditionally, the Panchayat had meant the council of five village elders who mediated conflict among the residents and who spoke on their behalf to their feudal authority. Questions of representing women or lower castes simply did not arise. In several parts of India, this body still exists as an informal instrument of governance. However, with India's emergence as a sovereign modern state, the gram (village) Panchayat (assembly) became the basic unit of democratic government because it is the first-level elected body covering at least 5,000 people. A GP may therefore encompass several villages or, in a specific locality, represent as many as 7,000. However, on average at this level, each council member represents some 400 citizens.

Unlike the imposition of female quotas "from the top" in the former Soviet Union and a number of other countries of Central and Eastern Europe, the Indian reform did not grow out of a rigorous theoretical base, such as Marxism. It also had a number of precedents from very different parts of the country. Moreover, the Constitutional amendment was coupled with a quota of 15 per cent for India's "scheduled" and "other backward" castes and tribes (SCs and STs)—for the most part, the "untouchables" of traditional Hinduism—of which women comprise half, but have no distinct political existence. All these factors, as well as others, account for the mixed results of the Panchyati raj (PRI) experiment to date. A glance at the past may therefore be useful, however oversimplified.

Background

The birth of modern India was strongly marked by Gandhian philosophy and the democratic socialism of Nehru and his associates in the Congress Party well

WOMEN'S POLITICAL PARTICIPATION AND GOOD GOVERNANCE: 21ST CENTURY CHALLENGES

---

[65] Poornima Vyasulu is Danida Advisor, Women in Agriculture Programme, Karnataka, India. Vinod Vyasulu is a Consulting Economist and Secretary, Centre for Budget and Policy Studies in Bangalore, India.

before the nation's independence in 1947. Although these two streams of thought differed at many points, they converged at others, including their mutual affirmation of the dignity and equality of women. The Constituent Assembly of 1946 numbered 16 women among its 150 members and immediately granted universal suffrage.

However, although the Constitution initially provided for the establishment of village councils, no state of the new Union was obligated to set up such a system of local self-government. Many saw this provision as a concession to Gandhi rather than as an urgent requirement for democracy that called for immediate implementation. Indeed, many in the Congress Party, Nehru among them, saw local elites and upper castes, especially in the rural areas, as so well-entrenched that emphasis on local self-government could only mean continued exploitation of the vast numbers of the downtrodden throughout India. Nation-wide, therefore, the distribution of power deliberately favoured the central government, in large measure to build national unity, but also because the country's first leaders felt that the educated elite (largely urban) that dominated the Congress Party would deal more justly—at least, more impartially—with the poor. To improve the lives of these new citizens socially and economically, the national government launched an immense community development programme with its own Ministry in the capital.

When the three-tiered Panchayati raj system was first launched in 1957, the committee that had prepared the bill recommended that GPs comprise two women "who are interested in work among women and children". Further, in 1961, the Panchayat Act of the State of Maharashtra provided for the "nomination of one or two women … in case women were not elected". West Bengal followed suit in 1973. In 1976, given the continued paucity of women in Panchayat institutions at all tiers, the national Committee on the Status of Women demanded women's representation in all these bodies, as well as the establishment of "All-Women Panchayats at the village level." Nonetheless, in most parts of India, women served officially almost entirely as proxies for their husbands, fathers and even sons, even where small quotas were mandated. In the meantime, it should be added, the nation-wide community development programme had markedly declined.

However, an enormous breakthrough for women came in 1983, when the southern state of Karnakata began reserving 25 per cent of Panchayat seats for women. Although elections were not held until 1987, some 14,000 women—80 per cent of them wholly new to political participation—were elected from 30,000 candidates. Women's representation remained poor in states that made no such provisions. In 1988, for example, Uttar Pradesh revealed a rate of less than 1 per cent. By contrast, in 1991 in Kerala, where 30 per cent of the seats had been reserved, 35 per cent of the district council seats were won by women. Similarly, in 1994 in Madhya Pradesh, with a 33 per cent quota, women captured 43 per cent of GP seats.

Regional Experiences

In a country as geographically and culturally diverse as India, the character of GPs naturally varies significantly, as do the women themselves. Indeed, in this connection, it should be noted that the 1993 Panchayat raj Amendment to the Constitution did not stem from any mass campaign spearhead by women's organisations or by grassroots movements. It resulted largely from the efforts of the Janata Dal, the political party that swept the country's national elections in 1989, to appear closer to the vast majority of India's people than the Congress Party that had hitherto ruled the country since independence. And, significantly, Janata Dal won its first notable victories in Karnataka in the early 1980s. Both decentralisation and the enlargement of women's political participation have thus been "top-down" revolutions closely bound to one another. Even as important a state as Bihar—one of India's poorest—has not yet held Panchayat elections under the new amendment.

Moreover, given the general centralizing trends in the Indian polity, the states too developed an authoritarian system of governance. State authorities tended to dominate the lower tiers of governance—or, more correctly, administration. At the state level generally, strong line departments took over development programmes. All the while, the bureaucracy grew in influence. Women were suddenly brought into this system as one dimension of this complex process—and it defines the context in which they have to function.

While this paper focuses on the PRI developments of Karnataka, it may be useful to look at that of other states, notably those that experimented with these institutions before the Constitution was

WOMEN'S
POLITICAL
PARTICIPATION
AND GOOD
GOVERNANCE:
21ST CENTURY
CHALLENGES

42

amended: Kerala, West Bengal, Andhra Pradesh, and Madhya Pradesh.

Kerala

Kerala has undertaken a wide variety of ventures in involving grassroots citizens in the planning process. But Kerala is exceptional in several ways, notably in its high levels of literacy and its history of political mobilisation. Moreover, in Kerala, the role of the party politics is a strong one and there is apparently an overlap between party functioning and patriarchal attitudes.

A recent study has shown that, in this state with high literacy, women who have held positions in the PRIs are not keen on contesting again. This is true in Karnataka as well. In both states, most of these women were new to political participation in 1993. Given the fact that their PRI peers and role models are largely men, do they fear becoming less feminine? Or are they afraid that they will have to abandon their advocacy for women and the issues that concern their women constituents most at the local level: health, education, sanitation, housing and related questions? Do they feel that further involvement in political life will inevitably mean becoming enmeshed in pervasive corruption? Different women have in fact voiced all these types of anxieties in one form or another. However, given the newness of the PRI experiment, it is too early to draw conclusions about any of these eventualities, or, more generally, about the rate of women's participation in politics at this level.

West Bengal

West Bengal introduced the PRI system in 1978 under its Marxist Left Front government, without, however, any special provision for women's representation in these bodies. Although PRIs have taken strong root throughout the state, charges of corruption persist in the newspapers and courts. A major reason for the activism of the PRIs appears to be due to the party cadres working within them; politically untrained Panchayat members would probably not have been equally effective. It is also worth noting that NGOs, in which many women are active, generally find themselves operating in a hostile environment in West Bengal, often against the PRIs. Overall, however, the situation of women within the local councils appears to be more satisfactory than that in other states.

Andhra Pradesh

Although Andhra Pradesh decentralised power to PRIs during the 1980s—with a proviso that 9 per cent of the seats be reserved for women (not, however, among the executive positions), the struggle for which the state is best known, the anti-arrack, originated not with PRI women, but those of an activist literacy programme in Nellore district modelled on the methodology of Paulo Freire, in which the abuses stemming from alcoholism (the rampant consumption of arrack) became a focal point of basic education in 1992. Students in the programme pushed for a policy of prohibition. Unfortunately, when the Telugu Desam Party won power in Andhra Pradesh by highlighting the efforts of these women, the state took over their campaign. The women subsequently became curiously disempowered and prohibition developed into a hotbed of corruption. Trapped in a situation, in which they had no control, the women's group disbanded. Little remains of the excitement of the literacy campaign days today.

Although the PRI system continues to exist in Andhra Pradesh, its current Chief Minister has introduced a centralised programme for rural development. It is based on projects proposed by local people themselves, who often contribute their labour in return for certain state inputs that they themselves cannot afford to buy. The programme explicitly seeks the involvement of women in deciding upon what is to be done and how the project will be implemented, managed and monitored, in accordance with clear state guidelines as to financing and in-kind inputs. Even the programme's critics say that it has led to significant improvements in the rural areas. Corruption also appears to have diminished significantly.[66]

Although this centralised programme exhibits a number of the benefits generally associated with decentralisation, it marginalises the PRIs—to the point where a number of their members recently conducted a fast in front of the Chief Minister's house. It would therefore appear that while much good development work can be done through the PRIs, many require assistance in efficient managerial techniques.

WOMEN IN THE PANCHAYATI RAJ: GRASSROOTS DEMOCRACY IN INDIA

---

[66] This draws on personal discussions with the field co-ordinators of the Gandhi Peace Centre, who have been working in several districts of AP and who have observed this programme closely.

Madhya Pradesh

By contrast with Andhra Pradesh, in Madhya Pradesh, the Chief Minister staked his political career on the PRI system. He had two advantages. First, none of the state's major parties were looking at decentralised governance in the countryside; their attention was fixed firmly on urban areas and large contracts. He left these issues to his Cabinet. Second, Constitutional amendment had just been adopted, elections had been held, and many newly elected local representatives were looking for work and responsibility.

Moreover, in Madhya Pradesh in 1995, the state authorities had just brought out the first state-level Human Development Report, which revealed that although every locality had a school, state literacy levels were abysmal, along with health and other social indicators. Accordingly, the Chief Minister set up the Rajiv Gandhi Missions—co-ordinated from his office—to improve the situation in close collaboration with PRI members. Each elected representative accompanied by the local school-teacher conducted a survey of education and other conditions in her or his constituency. The Mission Office provided the technical support. As a result, each representative developed a good idea of constituency needs and set priorities were set that would be met through the Rajiv Gandhi Missions coordinated from the Chief Minister's office.

Low literacy rates emerged as a result of inadequate access for many rural children who lived far from the local school. Accordingly, the state set up an Education Guarantee Scheme, which ensured instructional facilities for every roughly 40 children within any given Panchayat willing to provide space for a school and a local teacher trainee who had finished 12th standard. The government undertook to set up a school, provide materials and train the would-be teacher in pedagogy within 90 days. Funds were transferred directly to the district administration, which would supervise the functioning of the school.[67] Within two years, over 20,000 such schools were established.

Thus Madhya Pradesh has made use of the Panchayat system in an innovative way to meet social sector needs and now has perhaps the most progressive PRI system in the India. However, here as in the country as a whole, power has been given to people at the grassroots level by a government rather than as a result of their own demands. It nonetheless remains a positive development that must be built upon.

PRIs in Karnataka

As indicated earlier, Karnakata established its own PRI system in 1983 (with two tiers rather than the three stipulated a decade later by the Constitution) This initial reform reserved 25 per cent of local council seats for women before the national stipulation of one third in 1993. Since the third cycle of elections was scheduled for 1999, considerable experience had already accumulated.

In addition, starting in the early 1920s, the British Raj authorities throughout Mysore had begun taking action to improve the lives of the lower castes, having decided in 1918 that everyone in the province except the Brahmins and Christians was "backward". Although these reforms did significantly penetrate into the scheduled castes and tribes, which fell bellow the "other backward castes" [OBCs] in the traditional hierarchy, many men who had hitherto had little exposure to education and other benefits were therefore able to move up the social scale, a number entering the professions. Women also benefited indirectly.

This anti-Brahmin movement produced political power shifts that endure today, perhaps at the expense of the members of the scheduled castes and tribes (SCs and STs), since the OBCs predominate in the PRIs and, indeed, have their own quota in Karnakata. In the 5,640 GPs of the state, with a total of 80,627 seats, 17,906 are reserved for SCs, 7575 for STs and 26,828 for BCs. The open seats total 28,306 and many of those who enter the contests for them are OBCs. In short, earlier progressive legislation appears to have produced a backlash. Moreover, since caste and class in India, as elsewhere, are often at variance, some OBCs are affluent and some Brahmins below the poverty line.

To the extent that caste and gender overlap, the representation given to women has done little to change the caste hold on power. Upper caste women often vote and take other action along caste rather than gender lines. In the context of a drinking water problem, when one upper caste

---

67 See Vinod Vyasulu, "In the Wonderland of Primary Education" Report submitted to the Rajiv Gandhi Prathmik Siksha Mission, Bhopal, August 1998.

woman PRI member took up the cause of SCs in the case of a broken pipeline, she was publicly asked by female social peers why she was bothered to do so when she herself had water; the pipe break was, after all, "their" problem, not "ours".

At the gram Panchayat level in Karnataka, well over 40 per cent of the elected representatives are women. Many have come into politics for the first time. If they lack experience, they also have not been spoiled by past practices. However, as indicated at the beginning of this chapter, many are also illiterate, poor and landless. More than three-quarters are below 45 years of age—apparently because older women are more heavily shackled psychologically by tradition and therefore reluctant to enter politics. If the younger women emerge relatively unintimidated by the socio-economic obstacles they face, many can look forward to a long career in politics. However, many are surrogates for husbands and fathers who could not contest because of the imposition of the quota. Some were put in place by the wealthy and powerful for their to serve as puppets for particular vested interests. All these factor have led to problems widely discussed in the literature published since the amendment of the Constitution and captured in part in the UNICEF-sponsored film, *Shansodhan*.[68]

There have also been many efforts to train the newly elected women, several undertaken by the state government. The Karnataka Department of Women and Child Development co-operated with professionals in what has come to be known as the Gramsat Programme, part of which used satellite technology to link the different district headquarters interactively. The second part of the training material, developed as an extension of the satellite interchange, deals in large measure with issues in which women have indicated particular interest: nutrition, water, primary education, basic health services, immunizations and common property resources. Its impact has yet to be assessed.

One anecdote alone conveys a number of the problems faced by the vast majority of the newly elected women. In a GP with eight seats—and two positions reserved for SCs and one for STs—four of the members are women. When the elections were held in 1993, the village elders persuaded the voters to propose only one candidate for each post under the new system of quotas. The post of GP President having been reserved for an ST woman,

the only eligible candidate, a woman who had had only four years of formal schooling, was thus automatically chair. Moreover, she was neither a surrogate for a male member of her family nor a proxy member for any vested local interest. The other members did not mind her holding an ordinary seat, but could not accept her in this executive position and asked her to resign. This she was not willing to do. The others refused to co-operate with her.

Having sought the advice of the officials at higher levels, she found that she need not resign, that the quorum for meetings was three members, and that she and two other members could take decisions. With the help of the two SC members, she conducted several meetings and, when the others protested, she went to the High Court in Bangalore, which ruled in her favour. Nonetheless, the five protesting members refuse to abide by the Court's decision and attend every third meeting, signing the register to retain their membership and leaving immediately. Given this lack of co-operation, the President has had to work virtually alone in obtaining support at the higher levels for such basic public works as the digging of gutters and the construction of a bus stand.

In yet another GP, the election of an SC woman as President caused the resignation of all the other members and the suspension of village government functions for over a year. There are, of course, other GPs, as well as district councils, in which women have had considerable success—one SC woman having formed a woman's association that succeeded not only in accessing government loans, but in launching her election to higher tiers of government. However, a number of these "successful" women have served as proxies for men and/or have had far more education than the GP President of the story above. Her case alone poses a number of questions that remain to be answered throughout India:

Does a quota for women bring about social change? What is the relation between caste and class? Do quotas bring to prominence people who otherwise would never have attained governance positions? Would men have fared differently? Can higher officials legally intervene in the functioning of local governments so as to impose on village groups the authority of a person they have rejected? If so, what is the meaning of decentralisation and democracy? Where does "top down" cease and "bottom up" begin? What are the trade-offs among efficiency, efficacy, equity and equality?

---

[68] Directed by Govind Nihelani, and a staple in training courses now.

In Lieu of a Conclusion

The Panchayat raj institutions can influence existing social realities only slowly and to a limited extent.

The grinding poverty in which most of India's people live makes the ideals of democracy and ethics distant concepts. Their daily reality is exploitation of different sorts in which corruption is a matter of routine in which the payment of a bribe is seen largely as a minor nuisance to getting something done, however basic or superfluous that task may be.

The first Indian efforts at decentralisation were geared at little more than creating an efficient local tier of development administration was intended. This probably remains the primary desire of senior national government officials—and must constantly be borne in mind in any evaluation of the Panchayat raj reform. What is true of the national government also holds for the line departments of state governments, which still take the major decisions regarding rural life. Most of these state officials regard district postings and Panchayat authorities as nuisances. Moreover, the state bureaucracies tend to be even less gender-sensitive than their national counterparts. It is no accident that most of those who have been most enthusiastic about the PRI reforms are women who belong to the national urban elite.

The women who have come into the new system under caste quotas are, for the most part, functionally illiterate, with few productive assets; the vast majority depend on wage labour in a traditional rural society that has rigidly fixed places for various castes as well as for gender. None of these elements can be changed by constitutional amendments. To take a very rough parallel, the USA amended its Constitution to make ex-slave male African Americans full citizens during the late 1860s and its civil rights struggle still generates headlines, as does the 1920 Constitutional amendment that gave women the franchise and all the legal benefits of that right.

What Can Reasonably Be Expected of the PRI Reforms?

Because their survival is at stake, India's poor are accustomed to coping in a feudal type of system. Rural reality is complex; being freed from bondage often has not meant the freedom that many expected. Experience has taught them to proceed slowly and to approach their goals indirectly. They have to decide if attending PR meetings is sometimes worth missing their daily wages. This choice is even more important to women than to men.[69]

Moreover, they do not even know if the new PRI system is permanent. In West Bengal, two rounds of elections were needed before the system was accepted in the countryside. In Karnataka, constant tinkering with the system has meant that people are still cautious about using it. Why risk one's local position vis-à-vis powerful people if the system is again going to change?

The new system also coexists with traditional institutions that provide no space for women. These old councils of elders wield power in ways unforeseen by the Constitution—and, by virtue of the fact that they have no formal status, they are very difficult to change by law. If the PRIs are to succeed in their main goals, they must work in harmony with these traditional institutions, not confront them directly.

While giving women positions in the Panchayats is good in itself, it would be naïve to believe that it would address social injustice or issues of poverty. Gender as a phenomenon in itself rarely exists in a pure form anywhere in the world. How much more so, then, in India where gender is almost always alloyed with caste, class, and religious factors, any and all of which may clash, depending on the issue at stake?

Politics in India, as elsewhere in the world, can be a rapid vehicle for upward mobility. This is why the reservation of the posts of President to the SC/ST category is so resented, particularly for women. They can be members of the Panchayat, but not its President or Vice President. If they do occupy such posts, conflict between their caste and gender identities is almost inevitable. Different individuals will cope in different ways, forging alliances with other institutions that range from constitutional structures through political parties as they see fit in diverse circumstances. Politics, as always, is the art of the possible.

[69] The title of a recent book by Brinda Datta, dealing with women in PRIs, is *Who Will Make the Chapattis?*

WOMEN'S
POLITICAL
PARTICIPATION
AND GOOD
GOVERNANCE:
21ST CENTURY
CHALLENGES

What is the Relationship Between NGOs and PRIs?[70]

The early chapter of this volume on women's agency in governance asked much the same question in relation to formal government structures in general throughout the world. In India, as elsewhere, many NGOs work in the social sector and have strong links at the grassroots level, where they have little positive experience of government. Indeed, many of them became grassroots social activists because of government failures. Consequently, there are NGOs that resent the emergence of PRIs because they now have to vacate space for these new bodies. Some see PRIs as rivals for implementing government programmes and believe that they themselves are superior because they are not "political". By contrast, a number of NGOs have been involved in training those elected to PRIs and welcome the emergence of these local governments.

To date, certainly, the most valuable area of contribution of NGOs to engendering the PRIs has been the organizing of women in various social sectors, whether health, housing, sanitation, education or watershed management. The opportunities provided in small groups dealing with such issues has been a kind of testing ground for women to enter a larger arena after having been initially empowered. Various reports indicate that women PRI members who have been supported and nurtured by NGOs and those who have been involved in larger people's movements are more assertive than others. This is true even of the members of the vastly weakened Anti-Arrack movement in Andhra Pradesh.

Despite all these positive developments, most NGOs seem vary of becoming directly or even closely involved with the PRIs. Some may be bound by donor conditionalities; others may consider it wise not to confront the political establishment directly.

Yet if PRIs, especially GPs, are the forum where development and politics has to be wedded, it is difficult to see how NGOs can continue to be non-aligned in the politics of power transfer in the PRIs. The clearer their perspective on gender, the greater will be their contribution to the process.

BIBLIOGRAPHY

Bhat, M. K., D. Rajsekhar and N. Webster (1996). *People Centred Development-Panchayats and NGOs*, Bangalore Consultancy Office.

Chandrashekar, B. K. (1984). "Panchayati Raj Law in Karnataka: Janata Initiative in Decentralisation", *Economic and Political Weekly*, April 2,

_____ (1989). "Panchayati Raj Bill: The Real Flaw", EPW, July 1.

Das, S. K. (1998). *Civil Service Reform and Structural Adjustment*, Oxford University Press, New Delhi.

Datta, Brinda, (?). *Who Will Muke the Chapattis?*

Isham, Jonathan, D. Narayan and L. Pritchett (1995). "Does Participation Improve Performance? Establishing Causality with Subjective Data", *The World Bank Economic Review*, Vol. 9, No. 2, May.

Khilnani Sunil (1997). *The Idea of India*, Hamish Hamilton, London.

Palanathuri, G. (1999). "Women Participation in Local Governance— A Case Analysis of Tamil Nadu" Paper presented at a National Seminar on "Women in Local Governance: Exploring New Frontiers" February 3-6, 1999, ISST, Bangalore.

Pani, Narendar (1982). *Reforms To Pre-Empt Change*, Concept Publishers, Delhi.

Pushpa, Maitri (1993). 'Verdict', in *Katha III*, Rupa Publishers.

Subha, K. (1995). *Karnataka Panchayat Elections 1995*, Institute of Social Sciences, Bangalore.

Vyasulu, Vinod (1998a). "In the Wonderland of Primary Education" Report submitted to the Rajiv Gandhi Prathmik Siksha Mission, Bhopal, August.

_____ (1998b). "Give the system a Chance" *Deccan Herald*, October.

_____ (1998c). "Panchayats: NGOs or Local Governments?" unpublished paper, Bangalore, September.

_____ (1998d). "Panchayats: Local Government or NGOs?" Paper presented at a seminar at the Centre for Study of Culture and Society, Bangalore, November.

---

[70] See M. K. Bhat, D. Rajsekhar and Neil Webster, *People-Centred Development—Panchayats and NGOs*, Bangalore Consultancy Office, for a detailed discussion of this theme.

CHAPTER 6

THE SOUTH AFRICAN WOMEN'S BUDGET INITIATIVE

DEBBIE BUDLENDER[71]

Born in mid-1995, approximately a year after the country's first democratic elections, the South African Women's Budget Initiative evoked widespread interest not only domestically, but abroad in nations with vastly different franchise experiences. Within two years, a parallel government exercise began, led by the Department of Finance. Within three years the Initiative had produced three volumes that analysed all sectoral allocations of the government's budget from a gender perspective (Budlender, 1996, 1997, 1998), as well as a fourth book that translated parts of the comprehensive presentation into practical lay language (Hurt and Budlender, 1998).

A number of other countries, particularly in southern Africa have embarked on their own women's budgets. The Commonwealth Secretariat is providing assistance to three countries (South Africa being one) in gender budget analysis, and sees this activity as their first step in tackling the issue of gender and macroeconomics.

This short paper concentrates on South Africa's outside-government initiative—which has the longer experience—but refers to the inside-government exercise and the nature of the relationship between the two. It does so by focusing on the four following areas:

■ Methodology used to examine the gender impact of key aspects of the South African budget;
■ Theoretical framework for engendering the budget process;
■ Identification of key alternatives for reprioritization of budget issues; and
■ Examination of formal and informal alliances that contributed to the success of this initiative.

Methodology

The Women's Budget does not propose a separate budget for women. It examines the *whole* of the government budget to determine its differential impacts on women and men, girls and boys. Further, in South Africa, the exercise has emphasized differential impacts on differing *groups of women and men*, studying them along lines such as race, geography and income.

WOMEN'S POLITICAL PARTICIPATION AND GOOD GOVERNANCE: 21ST CENTURY CHALLENGES

[71] Debbie Budlender is editor and overall co-ordinator of the South African Women's Budget Initiatives, and works for the Community Agency for Social Enquiry, Cape Town, South Africa.

The Three Aspects of Gender Budget Analysis

The South African exercise was informed by the 15-year Australian experience in gender budget analysis (See Sharp and Broomhill, 1998). In particular, it adopted the framework proposed by Rhonda Sharp, an Australian economist who assisted both federal and state governments in the early years.

Sharp proposes that a gender budget analysis incorporate three aspects:

(a) **Gender-specific expenditures:** These consist of moneys allocated for programmes and policies that are specifically targeted on gender lines. These expenditures come closest to the way in which people usually first interpret the words "Women's Budget" in that they are separate and relatively easily distinguishable amounts. This aspect would, for example, include the Mozambican government's allocation for education of young women in technical subjects; the South African Department of Welfare's economic empowerment programme for unemployed mothers with children under five years; and staff, operating and programme costs associated with the various forms of gender machinery adopted by different countries.

(b) **Expenditures that promote gender equity within the public service:** These consist of monies allocated to affirmative action and other programmes that promote what in South Africa is termed greater "representivity" within the public service. Equity here would mean not only equal numbers of women and men employed, but equal representation within management and decision-making posts, equal representation across different occupations, and equitable pay and conditions of service. South Africa would look closely at race as well as gender and equity. The objective of such expenditures is, firstly, justice for the women and men employed and, secondly, a service that is more sensitive to the diversity of the population it serves.

WOMEN'S
POLITICAL
PARTICIPATION
AND GOOD
GOVERNANCE:
21ST CENTURY
CHALLENGES

(c) **Mainstream expenditures:** These consist of the remaining expenditures not covered by the first two categories. In the much better resourced Australian context, each of the first two categories accounted for at best 1 per cent of total expenditure. Unless this third category is addressed, a gender budget analysis will deal with what are essentially peripheral issues.

This third aspect of the analysis is not only the most important, but also the most difficult. To take a fairly simple example, in 1994, the education statistics of South Africa show that 20 per cent of African[72] women aged 20 years and above had no formal education whatsoever, as compared with 14 per cent of African men in this age group. Yet in the 1995/6 government budget, only approximately 1 per cent of the total allocated to education was to be spent on adult basic education and training (ABET). Meanwhile, 16 per cent of the total was to be spent on tertiary education, a sector with a similar potential student base in which women dominated at the distant education institutions rather than the more expensive residential ones—and where state subsidies in the male-dominated courses of study were higher than those in which women tended to congregate.

The Two Sides of the Budget

The South African Women's Budget, like other exercises to date, has concentrated on the expenditure side of the budget. The first book, however, included a chapter on taxation. By definition, ultimately as much money must be collected in revenue in any budget as is allocated as expenditure. Analysis of expenditure should therefore be included in gender budget analysis and needs to include all forms of revenue.

Policy-driven budgets

Gender budget analysis is based on an understanding that budgets should follow policy rather than vice-versa. Policy, in turn, should reflect the situation in the society. Simple as these assumptions may seem, the educational example cited above demonstrates the disparities between professed ideals and their implementation. Each sectoral analysis of the South African exercise typically begins by describing the gendered situation within a particular sector. It explains current gender, race and other patterns within the sector, as well as pointing out the particular relevance of the services concerned for women and men, girls and boys.

---

[72] As always, any meaningful analysis in the South African context is forced to adopt the racial classifications imposed during apartheid. These classifications can be opposed on both scientific and moral grounds. Nevertheless, they had very real effects on the people so classified. The African group was the largest one and also the one suffering from the heaviest discrimination and oppression. The other three groups, in diminishing order of disadvantage, were coloured, Indian and white.

This situation analysis is followed by a description of policy. In post-apartheid South Africa, there has been a plethora of new policy across all sectors. Given the overall commitment in the country to gender equity, as reflected in the Constitution's heavy emphasis on equality, most of these policies take some account of gender—or at least mention women. The analysis within the Women's Budget Initiative considers the extent to which this policy addresses the existing gender disparities.

At this stage, the analysis turns to the budget itself. Given a fair amount of existing gender analysis in the country, this is clearly where the real added value of the exercise becomes apparent. Here the question is the extent to which the budget reflects those policies which have been found to be gender-sensitive and appropriate. This reflects the central argument of the Initiative as to the centrality of the budget in determining effective government policy. Stated bluntly, the Initiative asserts that without adequate budgetary allocations, any policy, no matter how sensitive, will be ineffective.

Within government, the strong policy link implies that such initiatives will be most successful when carried out as a collaborative venture between staff from the policy, budget, information management system and gender units. To date such extensive intra-departmental collaboration has seldom occurred, either in South Africa or elsewhere.

Redistribution within limited resources

South Africa, like other countries, does not have infinite resources. Given its troubled history, South Africa's needs are magnified by severe inequalities in its society. These which extend from the income statistics usually quoted across access to virtually every type of service.

Limited resources and seemingly unlimited needs pose the classic economic problem of resource allocation. This is what budgets are all about. The Women's Budget Initiative openly acknowledges that these tensions exist and that resources are not infinite. Consequently, instead of simply arguing for "more", the Initiative tries to point out where savings can be effected so that "more" can be allocated to women or to gender-sensitive programmes and policies. In particular, it points to expenditures based on policies which might be subverting gender equity.

Timing

Timing is an important practical consideration in the methodology of policy-oriented research. The Women's Budget Initiative has timed its work so that each year the research is completed in time for Budget Day, when the national Minister of Finance tables the budget and accompanying documentation.

In the first year the research was launched at a full-day workshop on the Sunday before Budget Wednesday. The workshop was attended by parliamentarians, media people, NGO representatives and others and included plenary presentations as well as group discussions of sectoral findings. Because of the publicity, key stakeholders were aware of the initiative and some of the key findings at the time when government debate about the budget was most intense. The Select Committee on Finance also organised special hearings on women at which the Initiative, as well as other women's organisations, made presentations. Although no similar central workshop has taken place since, those involved in the Initiative have ensured that key people in each sector receive a copy of the reports. Further, in each year the findings have been presented in parliamentary post-budget hearings.

Although it reports at the time of the budget presentation, the outside-government analysis looks at the previous year's allocations. This is unavoidable because the new figures are available only on Budget Day. In practice this time-lag has to date been less of a drawback than might have been expected. Firstly, even in a country undergoing relatively rapid transformation, budgets generally change only marginally from year to year. Secondly, the detailed knowledge and overall understanding that researchers gain during the research process places them in a good position to pick up quickly on any changes, as well as their possible gender implications.

The time lag could become more of a problem as and when the Initiative returns to examine sectors previously researched. The Initiative will need to think whether and how it can draw on or complement the inside-government exercise in this respect. The problem might also be alleviated to the extent that government follows through on its initiatives in respect of multi-year planning and budgeting and greater involvement of civil society through earlier notification of key budget proposals.

THE SOUTH AFRICAN WOMEN'S BUDGET INITIATIVE

Theoretical Framework

"Women" and Gender

The name "Women's Budget" is a misnomer. A better name—and that chosen by the Tanzanian non-governmental initiative—is gender budget. The South African name misleads many people and generates opposition where it might not otherwise arise. Unfortunately, however, the Initiative has become known under the name and there is opposition from those involved to changing it at this stage.

Theoretically, the Initiative sees gender as defined by the social relations between women and men. These relations all too often reflect and result in inequities between women and men, but are by no means set in stone. If that were the case, there would be little sense in allocating money to try to change them. The Initiative's analysis recognizes further that all differences between women and men are unlikely to disappear. It sees the differences as constituting a problem only where they incorporate inequities.

The Initiative argues that government should allocate resources in a way that takes account of differential burdens borne and advantages enjoyed by women and men and try to balance these. The Initiative recognises that women are not always disadvantaged and that not all women are disadvantaged. Nevertheless, in the gendered relationship between women and men, all too often it is women who come off worse. In that sense, the "Women" in the title of the Initiative is attractive in bluntly stating the most common situation.

As indicated above, the South African Women's Budget Initiative has in three years produced an analysis of every sector of the government budget. Theoretically, the total coverage asserts that every aspect of society is gendered. This assertion was central from the outset. The Initiative started small, tackling only six sectors of expenditure in its first year. There was a strategic decision that those chosen should include a number of social sectors generally acknowledged as significant for gender and to which women would easily relate. In addition, the Initiative selected a number of less obvious sectors in order to illustrate how gender permeates all areas of society. The six sectors covered in the first year were thus Labour, Trade and Industry, the Reconstruction and Development Programme Office, Welfare, Housing and Education.

Unpaid Labour

A large proportion of the chapters of the three books raise the issue of unpaid labour. This reflects an underlying view of the economy different from that of traditional economists. The *Second Women's Budget* includes a chapter that provides the basis of an economic analytical framework more sensitive to gender issues.

Moreover, this focus on unpaid labour also reflects the work of Diane Elson (1997) and others on the "care economy". It challenges a view of the economy as composed of two producing sectors—private enterprise and government—with a third consuming sector comprising households. By contrast, it asserts that each of the three sectors consumes and produces. It points out, however, that the bulk of household production is unpaid and thus overlooked by economists because it seems to lack economic value. It points out that the bulk of this work is done by women. It shows the ways in which ignoring the effort and time spent on this work and the value of the goods and services produced by this work results in misallocation of resources—and of budgets in particular.

Methodological Diversity

The Initiative has drawn on a wide range of people from different sectors, disciplines and backgrounds to undertake the research which lies at its heart. While all advocate gender equity, their understanding of this concept and others may differ in some important respects.

The Initiative has encouraged all researchers to focus on "facts" more than on abstract theoretical arguments. Nevertheless, theory and ideology obviously underly the facts a researcher finds significant and how she or he presents and interprets them. The Initiative has not insisted on a tight and consistent theoretical or ideological approach from all its researchers. In the first workshops with researchers, the basic approach and key concepts utilised in the Initiative are presented and discussed. Afterwards, as a new undertaking in a largely unexplored field, the Initiative has encouraged experimentation. This flexibility caters better to the differences between sectors in their intrinsic nature, as well as factors such as availability of data and the existence of previous research. It also encourages the development of new techniques of analysis.

Key Alternatives for Re-prioritization

Because a short paper such as this cannot hope to cover all alternatives suggested by more than 20 authors analyzing some 30 allocations, it provides instead a few examples that suggest the range of *types* of alternatives that have emerged over the past years.

Most of the alternatives suggested in the Women's Budget Initiative reflect new priorities and emphases rather than wholly new ideas. It responds simply to the plethora of White Papers on a wide range of policies produced by the post-apartheid government, many of them often designed without sufficient (if any) attention to the resource requirements. Although the Department of Finance recently stipulated that all legislative proposals be accompanied by an estimate of the cost of implementation, the absence of such a practice in the past necessitated positing most of the "alternatives" discussed here and in the Women's Budget in terms of existing proposals.

Education

As discussed briefly above, one of the clearest examples of gender-biased expenditure is found in education. As in so many other countries, this sector accounts for the largest proportion of the government budget. Approximately 85 per cent of the total allocated to expenditure go to primary and secondary education. In comparison with many other Southern African countries, South Africa has high levels of enrolment, although the quality of the education and success rates of scholars is often poor. Like several other Southern African countries, there are slightly more girls than boys enrolled in schools. Further, given limited subject choice in most schools formerly destined for Africans, the subject differences between girls and boys are small.

Higher education accounts for 16 per cent of the government education budget. At this level, too, the number of women now exceeds the number of men. However, there are distinct gender patterns in the courses of studies followed. Men predominate at the *technikons*, which teach more technical subjects. Overall, women outnumber men at the universities, but they congregate at the distance learning institutions and in teaching and the "softer" social disciplines. Men generally predominate in

areas to which greater state allocations go—subjects increasingly favoured in education and science and technology statements and which generate higher incomes in later life for their graduates.

Three other points should be made about higher education in South Africa. First, it still features severe racial inequalities. Second, the state allocation for each higher education students is many times the size of the average allocations at any other level. Third, proposals for a graduate tax to cover some of the interim private cost of education at this level have been floated for several years without apparently receiving serious consideration by those in power. These proposals acknowledge that many students and their families do not have the requisite funds at the time they start studying. After graduating, however, these ex-students have incomes well above average. The general suggestion is that the government subsidizes students while they are studying, but reclaim the money afterwards through a surcharge on all taxpayers with tertiary qualifications.

Adult basic education and training (ABET) and pre-school provision each receive only about 1 per cent of the education budget, despite widespread illiteracy and proven benefits of pre-school provision for children, poor children in particular. The benefits of such provision for women are also obvious in their ability to free women to perform other tasks, as well as to provide income for women childcare practitioners. Nevertheless, government provision in eight of the country's nine provinces is restricted to a single school preparatory year, and in most cases focuses on formal sites that favour privileged areas.

Given all the foregoing factors, a gender-sensitive budget would clearly require re-prioritization in educational spending away from the tertiary level and towards ABET and early childhood development.[73]

Public works programmes

In some cases the re-prioritization required concerns the amount allocated far less than its targeting—whom this amount reaches. Here, examples would include the country's special employment programmes. The Public Works Department runs a nation-wide community-based public works

THE SOUTH AFRICAN WOMEN'S BUDGET INITIATIVE

---

[73] Early childhood development is the preferred name for what in other countries might be called "educare" or pre-school education. Early childhood development is thought to provide a better reflection of the need for a wide range of developmental inputs, including education and care.

programme that aims to build basic infrastructure in rural areas at the same time as providing short-term employment and training opportunities. The Department of Water Affairs and Forestry provides short-term employment opportunities when it builds new water supply and sanitation projects. The Department of Water Affairs and Forestry also co-ordinates a Working for Water programmes in which unemployed people are employed in eradicating algae and other vegetation to improve overall water conservation and supply.

These three programmes all provide short- or medium-term employment primarily for people with limited or no formal skills. All are labour-intensive and require relatively heavy physical labour. The programmes target similar communities: largely rural and, because of past policies of migrant labour and influx control, largely female among the adults. Despite these similarities, the three programmes have performed very differently in terms of providing jobs for women and men. A national evaluation of the community-based public works programme found that just over 40 per cent of those employed were women. However, women tended to be employed on the more menial jobs. Further, while 37 per cent of the employed men received training, only 32 per cent of the women did. The Department of Water Affairs and Forestry estimated that in 1997 about 14 per cent of those employed and 16 per cent of those who received training on the water and sanitation projects were women, despite the fact that Departmental policy has stipulated from the beginning that over half of all the workers on the Working for Water Programme be women.

Given these factors, gender-sensitive re-prioritization of these public works expenditure allocations would involve ensuring that the first two programmes adopt the methods employed by Working for Water to ensure that they, likewise, provide both immediate income-earning opportunities in the form of jobs and future income-enhancing opportunities in the form of training to those who need them most.

Trimming the Fat

A third type of re-prioritization involves reduction in the waste and inequalities that still exist in post-apartheid South Africa's government expenditure. Salary expenditures are among the most obvious—though certainly not the only—cases in which scarce resources appear to be misspent. Staff imbalances

are particularly worrying, given the government's commitment to "right-sizing", often crudely translated into downsizing.

One of the more startling examples is the staff complement serving the President. Examination of the budget of the Office of the President revealed that in addition to the 108 office staff, the budget allowed for 82 staff members within the President's household, including 61 cleaners, three food services aides, eight household aides, a general foreman, a storekeeper, three household managers, one guest house manager, two household supervisors and two household controllers. The salary of each of these individuals would provide monthly child support grants of R100 for a great number of children.

Alternatively, the amounts could be used to increase the already over-stretched complement of inspectors charged with enforcing the Basic Conditions of Employment Act, which provides for minimum standards in relation to work hours, overtime, contracts and related matters—and which has recently been extended to cover to the hundreds of thousands of women employed as domestic workers. Even before the extension, the Department of Labour's inspectorate was too small to provide adequate inspection and enforcement. With the sudden increase in the number of workers covered, and with most of these workers in separate work-places, the demands on the inspectorate will multiply.

More generally, the highest government officials are still earning very high salaries. In 1993, the ratio between highest and lowest pay in the public service was around 25:1. By 1996 this ratio had fallen to 16:1. Although the gap has been reduced, it is still unnecessarily high by international norms, which range between 10 and 20 to 1. In addition to consuming large amounts of money, these gaps disadvantage women relative to men. In 1997, approximately half of all public servants were women—only 27 and 38 per cent of them at the national and provincial levels respectively employed at director level or above. Women thus predominated among the service providers, but had relatively little decision-making power as to which services should be delivered and how.

Defence

Many budget advocacy projects focus on defence expenditure. The Women's International League for Peace and Freedom, one of the projects that have brought together the issues of budgets, women and defence, has made arguments such as the one above in respect of salary expenses concerning alternative uses for the amounts currently spent on expensive weapons and military machinery.

The South African Women's Budget Initiative tackled the defence sector only in its third year of research. This delay was the result of a conscious strategic choice. First, the Initiative wanted to excite interest by raising new arguments rather than giving people what they might automatically assume would emerge from such an exercise. Second, even before 1994, South Africa had started making dramatic cuts in defence expenditures—all in all, more than 9 per cent in the total national budget between 1989 and 1997/8, falling to 6 per cent in the 1997/8 budget.

Nevertheless, the chapter on defence in *The Third Women's Budget* revealed stark mismatches between the situation in the country, the policy statements and available resources. The chapter argues strongly that the major threat to South African security now comes from inside the country, in the form of poverty and inequality. To the extent that the military argues that they assist in maintenance of internal peace and security, resources should rather be allocated to sectors such as the police, which have the specialised skills and capacity to deal with these issues. For the most part, however, the country should be reallocating resources from maintaining internal security forces to the sectors that "attack" poverty and inequality economically and socially.

Formal and Informal Alliances

Parliamentarians and Non-governmental Organisations

The South African Women's Budget has an alliance at its heart in some of the "new" parliamentarians who entered parliament for the first time in 1994 who came together with representatives of two non-governmental organisations. The parliamentarians were members of the Joint Standing Committee on Finance, which spanned the National Assembly and then Senate. They were also eager to ensure that they carried forward their involvement in gender struggle and the more general struggle for equality in their new roles. The two NGOs were involved in policy analysis—one with a specific focus on budgets and the other with experience of gender and social policy analysis.

The two sides of the partnership have been important in ensuring the success of the Initiative to date. The non-governmental organisations have been able to provide the expertise and time necessary to collect information, undertake the research and produce the analysis. The parliamentarians have provided access to information and focus in terms of key political issues. Further, without the parliamentarians' strong advocacy voice, the analysis might well have remained to gather dust on the shelves or circulated and been used only within a closed circle of gender activists.

Involving a Wide Range of Actors

The Initiative's formal alliances extended beyond these particular types of people. The researchers were drawn from a range of other non-governmental organisations, academic institutions and elsewhere. They were also chosen for their knowledge of a particular sector and of gender issues rather than their knowledge of budgets.

The researchers were supported by a reference group—again, chosen for their knowledge of particular sectors. They included parliamentarians, government officials, members of non-governmental organisations and others who were too busy to do the research themselves, but who instead provided information and insights as they learned how to combine sectoral, gender and budget analysis in the process as a whole.

The individuals involved as researchers and members of the reference group changed each year. In adopting this approach, the Initiative was able to benefit from a wider field of experience and reach a wider group of people. Its reaching out also inspired initiatives from other interest groups that have investigated or plan to investigate the impact of the budget on groups such as children, rural people, the disabled, and the poor. Those so inspired have generally drawn on the expertise and advice of people involved in the Women's Budget.

The Initiative has made a conscious effort to extend the network of people involved in the project itself. It has, for example, not chosen researchers and reference group members only from people known to the core actors. Instead, through a snowballing reference process, it has drawn on people from a wide range of institutions and from many different areas of the country. Further, while most of the first year's researchers

THE SOUTH
AFRICAN
WOMEN'S
BUDGET
INITIATIVE

were white, over the years the Initiative has drawn on black researchers outside of what could have become largely closed circles.

Collaborating in Support for Reforms

Many of the Initiative's informal alliances reflect its support for existing proposals in respect of budget reform and other policy. For example, the South African government, like many others, is currently trying to move towards performance budgeting. A central tenet of performance budgeting measuring performance not only in monetary, but in physical terms. Performance budgeting requires that one looks firstly at *inputs*. These would include financial, human and other resources allocated to a particular programme or policy. Secondly, one looks at *outputs*, the physical deliverables of the programme or policy and the number of beneficiaries reached. Finally, one studies outcomes. These measure the impact of the policies and programmes on the situation and well-being of citizens, for example in their levels of health, income or education.

Government policies and expenditures will usually have a noticeable effect on outcomes only in the medium- to long-term. Further, a particular outcome is usually effected by a range of different policies and external factors. Expenditures and outcomes are therefore difficult to match.

A more realistic task in moving beyond detailing only human and financial inputs is to measure and monitor outputs. It is here that the gender budget initiative is in line with a reform close to the heart of the Department of Finance. The Initiative however, advocates an extra dimension in this reform by requiring gender and other disaggregations of the outputs. Fortunately, many people outside the Initiative have recognised the importance of this requirement. At heart performance budgeting is about ensuring that government expenditure is efficient—that one is getting value for the inputs allocated. Disaggregation of outputs ensures that the expenditure is efficient in the sense of being well-targeted. It also allows monitoring of the equity of allocations. Such monitoring should be important to both government and civil society players.

Fluidity

The fluid situation in South Africa has contributed to the Initiative's range of alliances. Since 1994,

those who previously worked together in opposition organisations have entered a wide range of previously undreamed-of positions. There are thus close networks that extend from cabinet ministers through parliamentarians and government officials at all levels to key non-governmental people. Further, because women were involved before 1994 in virtually all oppositional organisations, the links allow gender activists to reach a wide range of people who were and are less vocal in respect of gender issues.

The major movement into the new positions occurred in the first years after the 1994 elections. Throughout the life of the Initiative, however, additional moves have increased its influence— among these, the appointment of the current Deputy Minister of Finance, Gill Marcus, previously the chairperson of the Joint Standing Committee of Finance, who had been very supportive of the Initiative as chairperson and who, in her new position, has championed the inside-government exercise. The current Deputy Minister of Trade and Industry, also a strong supporter of the Initiative when it was first launched, has since encouraged the Department to utilize the findings of the Initiative's research, particularly in respect of small, medium and micro-enterprises. Maria Ramos, now Director-General (Principal Secretary) of Finance, was a senior official in the Department when the Initiative was first launched and served on the reference group for the first two years and is now the senior official ultimately responsible for the inside-government initiative. Neva Seidman Makgetla, now deputy Director General of the Department of Public Service and Administration, was with a non-governmental research organisation when she first served as reference group member, an official in the Department of Labour when she co-authored one of the chapters of the second book, and now at only one removed from the highest level of responsibility for the entire civil service.

Lessons Learned

Patience

The first and probably most important lesson of the Women's Budget Initiative to date is that there is no quick, easy recipe for undertaking gender analysis of the budget. Budgets have always been regarded as gender-neutral instruments and have been drawn up as such. They were not designed to

WOMEN'S POLITICAL PARTICIPATION AND GOOD GOVERNANCE: 21ST CENTURY CHALLENGES

reveal a variety of disaggregations. Determining the impacts requires not only hard work and perseverance, but also imagination.

Nor will this type of initiative result in rapid change. The first round of analysis usually reveals little more than gaps in knowledge. In the medium term, achievements seem to lie largely in the processes and procedures for putting in place gender-disaggregated data on outputs and specifying gender-aware targets. Quick changes in policy are few and far between and benefits in outcomes even slower.

Parallel Efforts

In Australia, the gender budget exercise was confined to the government, without lobbying from the outside, and has gradually diminished to a public relations exercise. The South African Initiative drew strength from being located both inside and outside government—and, outside government, from the collaboration between parliamentarians and non-governmental organisations. The latter the effective use of research, accompanied by powerful arguments, in lobbying and advocacy in powerful places.

Virtually no government can be expected to produce a cutting critique of its own activities. At most, it can be required to report honestly on what it is doing, what it hopes to do, and what difficulties it is experiencing in achieving its aims. Those outside government can utilize this information to suggest alternatives because they are freer to experiment both methodologically and politically.

Practical Experience

Gender budget analysis is best learned through practical engagement. Experience inside South Africa and in disseminating the ideas to other countries has demonstrated the importance of incorporating practical experience in helping people to understand what gender budget analysis is about. In most countries, gender training for civil servants—where it exists at all—is fairly general. Participants are rarely required to look beyond the difference between sex and gender, the differing roles of women and men, and their own prejudices and stereotyping practices. Even those who emerge from such training convinced and committed are unsure how to translate their convictions into daily work, particularly in the more specialised sectors that seem remote from gender concerns. Gender

budget training provides an opportunity for specialists to apply these concerns, even in very small ways.

Penetrating All Spheres and Levels of Government

South Africa has three spheres of government: national, provincial and local. The powers of different spheres of government are determined by the Constitution. The national sphere is responsible for overall policy formation, and for most of the security and economic functions such as police, defence, and affairs and trade and industry. The provincial sphere is responsible for the bulk of the major basic social services such as health, education, water and sanitation, and electricity. The local sphere is particularly weak in the more impoverished rural areas, most of which have no tax base of their own and are completely dependent on grants from other spheres.

In its first three years the South African Women's Budget Initiative focused on national and, to a lesser extent, provincial governance. Only in 1998, in response to many requests from local councilors and others, did the Initiative undertake pilot research on local government budgets. It concerns five of the 800 existing municipalities—one large city, two middle-sized towns, and two very rural councils—spread across four of the nine provinces. It is hoped that this sample will provide some indication of the diversity of the country's situations. Much of this research concerns the training of local councilors. The Initiative plans to produce a popular book on local government soon after the research is completed, so that local councilors (many of whom have minimal education), as well as others can use the findings and methods in their own areas.

Donor Funding to Government

Compared to other Southern African countries the South African government derives only a small proportion—about 2 per cent—of its revenue from outside sources, some 30 donors that comprise individual countries as well as multilateral institutions. Unlike many other developing countries, South Africa does not include these amounts when reporting on its budget.

While the total amount of aid is small, the omission may slant the overall picture. Anecdotal evidence suggests that aid is concentrated on certain sectors, such as education, and on certain geographical areas. These include both the most advanced, which are seen as more likely to use the money efficiently, and the poorest. The more "average" areas may meanwhile be losing out.

The Women's Budget research will attempt to reveal these biases, as well as any specific gender ones. The Initiative hopes that the research will add to the still muted calls for amending budgeting formats to include these revenues. Until that is done, those inside and outside government will be less able to judge accurately how well they are prioritizing and targeting the people and issues intended.

Widening the Audience

The production of popular material reflects a growing realisation within the Initiative of the need to make its materials accessible to a wider audience. As noted above, one of the downfalls of the Australian experience was the lack of pressure and interest from outside government. In South Africa the danger of low civil society involvement is increased by the low levels of economic and general literacy in the country. Within civil society, the Initiative runs the danger of being confined to a relatively small elite.

However, many of the researchers within the Initiative come into the project fearing inadequacy in dealing with figures and budgets, but soon shed these anxieties as their involvement grew. Those without the close involvement and the support provided by the Initiative may lack the incentive to press beyond their apprehensions. The popular books on the initiative will address this problem to some extent. Given a limited reading culture as well as the limited education of most South Africans, it is unlikely that these publications will reach the full potential audience, defined broadly as all organised women (and some men), whatever the forms of their organisations.

The Initiative plans to work with the Gender Education and Training Network (GETNET), an NGO that brings together gender trainers country-wide, to develop materials for use both in focused gender budget workshops and for sessions in other training events. The collaborative materials development process will include a training-of-trainers component that will produce a core team

of people who can take the message further. The materials themselves will complement the more detailed and technical material contained in a gender budget manual developed for government officials under the auspices of the Commonwealth Secretariat's gender budget project (Budlender, Sharp and Allen, 1998).

A Unique Case?

All cases are unique because all governments and cultures differ. Despite the very special circumstances under which the South Africa Women's Budget Initiative developed, the alacrity with which other counties have introduced their own gender budget initiatives suggests that South Africa's experience is, in large measure, replicable.

Of course, comparable initiatives in various countries differ on many counts: in their scope (which sectors are addressed, whether revenue is included, whether the exercise focuses only on national budgets, etc.); in respect of site (whether they occur inside government, within parliament, within non-governmental organisations, within academia, or across a range of such institutions); and in method and level of technical detail. These differences are natural because the budget is an intensely national issue; it reflects the overall policy and priorities of a government and its people. Further, such differences are fruitful, particularly in these early years of development and experimentation, when countries can share with each other their failures and successes in determining what is being allocated and how these patterns contribute to or remedy gender injustice.

BIBLIOGRAPHY
Budlender, Debbie (ed.) (1996) *The Women's Budget*, Institute for Democracy in South Africa, Cape Town.
_____(1997). *The Second Women's Budget*, Institute for Democracy in South Africa, Cape Town.
_____(1998). *The Third Women's Budget*, Institute for Democracy in South Africa, Cape Town.
Budlender, Debbie, R. Sharp and K. Allen (forthcoming). *How to do a gender-sensitive Budget analysis: Contemporary research and practice* Australian Agency for International Development and the Commonwealth Secretariat.
Elson, Diane (1997). "Gender-Neutral, Gender-Blind, or Gender-Sensitive Budgets? Changing the conceptual framework to include women's empowerment and the economy of care" Preparatory Country Mission to Integrate Gender into National Budgetary Policies and Procedures, London: Commonwealth Secretariat.
Hurt K. and D. Budlender (1998). *Money Matters: Women and the government budget*, Institute for Democracy in South Africa, Cape Town.
Sharp, Rhona and R. Broomhill (1998). "Government Budgets and Women: Shaking the foundations?" in M. Sawer (ed.) *Policy Makers and Policy Shakers*, Allen and Unwin, Sydney.

CHAPTER 7

ALLIANCES FOR GENDER AND POLITICS: THE UGANDA WOMEN'S CAUCUS

THE HON. BENIGNA MUKIIBI[74]

Since 1986, after the two decades of political strife and turmoil that followed Uganda's independence, a process of democratisation has been under way. As one participant observed, "This period [of guerrilla warfare] was a turning point for Ugandan women and men because new stakeholders, women, peasants and youth in particular, began to assert themselves and play roles they had never played before. Attitudes were changing towards leadership and towards women as well."

In 1994, a Constituent Assembly worked to create a new constitution for the country. According to an affirmative action measure decreed by the National Resistance Movement (NRM) government, a minimum of 15 per cent of those elected to Parliament and the Constituent Assembly—as well as one in nine local government council members—were to be women. When the Assembly convened, women delegates found themselves 51 in a total group of 284. Of these 51, 39 had been elected to affirmative action seats, while 9 had won in contested constituencies. These women also included two presidential nominees and one workers' delegate.

The Women's Caucus

To increase their political clout and broaden the base of support for women's issues, the women in the Constituent Assembly created a "Women's Caucus" and embarked on a series of strategic alliances. Within the Assembly, women joined with representatives of youth, workers, and disabled persons' delegates— a particularly important category because of the human destruction wrought by continuous civil strife directly and by its effects on health throughout the country. With impetus from six women delegates who called themselves the "Gender Working Group", women established an alliance known formally as "The Constituent Assembly Women's Caucus, Working with Youth, Workers, and People with Disabilities (PWD)." The Caucus was strictly non-partisan in nature and took positions only on issues of fundamental importance to women,

WOMEN'S POLITICAL PARTICIPATION AND GOOD GOVERNANCE: 21ST CENTURY CHALLENGES

---

[74] The Hon. Benigna Mukiibi, is Member of Parliament and member of the Forum for Women in Democracy (FOWODE) Kampala, Uganda. This paper was first presented at the Huairou Commission Best Practice Task Force Meeting, 1-3 February 1999, Mumbai, India.

youth or the disabled. In addition, membership was voluntary and informal. Nonetheless, all the women delegates to the Assembly considered themselves members.

As relative outsiders to the political process, Caucus participants quickly recognised their need for skills training. With support from USAID and the Ministry of Gender and Community Development (headed by a woman), they held numerous workshops for members, particularly on advocacy. Other topics on which they received training were managing campaigns and campaign strategy, constituency building, coalition building, speech-making and parliamentary procedures. Occasionally the Caucus received financial support to send members to regional or international conferences on specific issues of interest.

The Caucus also developed a working relationship with Uganda Women Lawyers, a professional association that provided them with comments on the provisions of the Constitution. To interact with Ugandan women at large, they learned from a prominent women's NGO, Action for Development (ACFODE), what grassroots women's organisations were saying through radio and TV broadcasts of their meetings. In return, Caucus members broadcast a weekly radio programme in which they examined issues under debate in the Constituent Assembly. The programme gave greater visibility to the Caucus and its work and, at the same time, provided community women with a sense of the give-and-take of politics in a democratic system. Additionally, the Caucus regularly invited representatives of the National Association of Women's Organisations of Uganda to participate in events in which Caucus policy decisions were shaped.

Gender Dialogues

As the work of the Constituent Assembly progressed, Caucus members identified certain issues as fundamental to their interests—among these, utilizing gender-neutral terminology throughout the Constitution and framing a constitutional provision that specifically declared equality between men and women under the law. To ensure that these and similar principles were included in the new Constitution, the Caucus held a series of "Gender Dialogues," to which they invited men and other non-caucus members, such as experts on the particular issue from the Friedrich Ebert Foundation.

Its coordinator of the Caucus, the Hon. Winnie Karagwa Byanyima, summed up the strategy of the Dialogues as follows: "Dialogues were given high profile and were always followed by a reception. This ensured a good turnout for discussion and, increasingly, male delegates wanted to be associated with these events and with our positions. Inviting non-members of our Caucus to take a position with us on an issue made the lobbying process much easier, because we used the non-members with whom we had agreed to advance the arguments to their colleagues and often we asked a non-member to move the Caucus amendment. It diffused potential oppositions."

Whenever a position was taken in the Dialogue, a brochure was issued to all the Assembly delegates to inform them and lobby them for support. Gender Dialogues were therefore the basic tools for building consensus, and were a great success.

Achievements

The Women's Caucus worked effectively as a minority in the Assembly. The Constitution was written in gender-neutral language; an explicit statement of equality before the law was included in the new Constitution; the principle of equality must now be written into the laws to be passed by the new Parliament in specific areas. The new Constitution explicitly prohibits laws, cultures, traditions or customs that undermine the dignity and well-being of women—a particularly important provision because of the many inherited cultural and traditional constraints that subordinate women and exclude them from the decision-making process.

In addition, the Caucus successfully lobbied for an Equal Opportunities Commission to guarantee enforcement of the Constitutional principle, and will be watching carefully to ensure that it receives adequate funding and the necessary autonomy.

Another important achievement of the Women's Caucus was expanding the scope of affirmative action and ensure its inclusion in the new Constitution. The 39 affirmative action seats in Parliament (about 14 per cent) may therefore be supplemented by others because the Caucus won the explicit right of women to contest all other seats. In addition to the original NRM decree, women are now guaranteed one third of local council seats. This latter provision will give more women political experience and an increasingly important role as Uganda's decentralisation of political authority progresses.

Lessons Learned

One key to the success of the Women's Caucus was its early acknowledgement of the need for alliances described above. Another vital ingredient its leadership's insistence on a non-partisan approach—not an easy task, as many Caucus members were attached to political parties whose male leadership attempted to inject partisan politics into Caucus work. The Caucus leadership found that constantly identifying and articulating its common agenda helped to counter these tendencies, as well as to remind members not to attempt to press other on issues that could not win consensus. When issues proved potentially divisive, the Caucus opted not to take a public stance rather than jeopardize its unity.

Caucus leaders also found that moving cautiously and thereby avoiding mistakes was a key to effective political action. On a lighter note, they discovered that Caucus activities were most effective when they had a high profile and were enjoyable. Most politicians benefit from publicity. This is no less true for women, particularly those who may be less known at the national level. And because political work is stressful, an activity that offers both favourable publicity and a degree of relaxation is a welcome break for Uganda's busy women in politics. It helped the Caucus function as a unified group.

After the completion of the Constituent Assembly, the Caucus members and others formed a new organisation, Forum for Women in Democracy (FOWODE), now a registered NGO with a small reference library and permanent staff. FOWODE's aim is to provide support and training for women and other marginalised groups as they seek to become involved in decision-making positions. The Forum has provided training services to women parliamentarians and activists in several Sub-Saharan countries including Botswana, Malawi, Namibia, Rwanda, South Africa and Zambia. Uganda's success in forming and sustaining a women's caucus has contributed to the establishment of comparable groups in these countries.

Local Government Project

Since 1995, FOWODE has been engaged in building the capacity of women leaders at the grassroots level. After the adoption of the new Constitution, FOWODE conducted seminars throughout the country to educate local government women leaders about their constitutional civic and human rights. Some 200 women local leaders were trained. The programme also introduced women leaders to the new structures of local government, the three branches of government (the executive, legislative and judiciary) and areas of the Constitution that deal with concerns of women and children. The programme was well received throughout the five regions of the country.

FOWODE has also trained over 600 women leaders in skills for participation in public life, including local government elections. A candidates' training package developed for this project by FOWODE was so successful that it has since been used as a training tool for women leaders in other African countries. Some of the women who contested local government seats won powerful positions, among them sub-country chairperson, executive offices in the district/sub-country executive committees, and chairs of standing committees.

FOWODE is also implementing a two-year programme for the women, youth and disabled councilors at district and sub-country levels who came into office in local government elections. The aim of this programme is to equip these councilors with skills to enable them participate effectively in their respective legislative bodies and to deliver constituency services.

Parliamentarians' Training Project

Under this project, FOWODE began by holding workshops to prepare women, youth and people with disabilities candidates for general elections held in June 1996 to enhance their capacity to organise and manage campaign teams; to identify and communicate issues to the electorate; and to raise funds in preparation for the elections. The training resulted in the participation of a greater number of women than those in earlier elections improved the quality of their campaigns. Most of

ALLIANCES
FOR GENDER
AND POLITICS:
THE UGANDA
WOMEN'S
CAUCUS

the women who were trained competed favourably, many winning election even to non-quota seats.

Upon their election, FOWODE launched a two-year skills training programme for Parliamentarians, providing training, information and library services to women MPs and MPs representing PWDs, Youth and Workers aimed at equipping these Parliamentarians with skills to enable them participate effectively in Parliament and to deliver constituency services. The Forum also initiated the formation of a Special Interest Groups (SIG), similar to the Women's Caucus, that includes all women MPs who represent workers, people with disabilities and the youth, along with an association of Gender-Sensitive Men (GSM) to enable these categories pursue their agenda in Parliament and ensure advocacy for gender concerns.

Engendering Ugandan Politics

All in all, the Women's Caucus has succeeded in incorporating gender perspectives into much important legislation. It has done so through public dialogues where key stakeholders, including representatives of women organisations, are invited to discuss pending legislation with Parliamentarians. These public dialogues have proved to be a powerful and effective advocacy tool. They give the public at large and particular interest groups an opportunity to contribute to Parliamentary debates and to lobby MPs for their interests. They also enable members of the SIG Caucus, to bend their views towards a consensus and have greater impact in Parliament.

Through such dialogues, the SIG Caucus was able to introduce gender sensitivity as an objective in the Local Government Act (Article 2 (c) of the Bill; election by universal adult suffrage (as opposed to electoral colleges) for the special women's seats in local government; and removal of an educational requirement for candidates that had disqualified most rural women from running for office. In the Land Act, too, the Caucus moved a variety of amendments that augmented the security of women in land tenure, notably safeguards for the rights of women and children (Article 28); written consent of the spouse before disposal of land (Article 40); and the provision of a quota for women and marginalised groups in Communal Land Association and District Land Boards.

The SIG Caucus has also reached consensus on the need to reform the current budget process. FOWODE's next objective therefore is empowering Caucus members to influence resource allocations at the national level in favour of poor women, young people, PWDs and other marginalised groups. The Ministry of Gender, Labour and Social Development has been training senior and middle-level government officials in gender responsive development planning and has also assisted several districts to mainstream gender concerns in their policies. Through the first steps of its Gender Budget Project, its next major endeavour, FOWODE will complement this national effort by working in two of these districts to introduce the skills required for ensuring that gender-sensitive policies are reflected in local budgets. Perhaps nowhere can it have greater impact for achieving democracy throughout Uganda.

WOMEN'S
POLITICAL
PARTICIPATION
AND GOOD
GOVERNANCE:
21ST CENTURY
CHALLENGES

62

CROSSING THE GOVERNANCE PRIVATE THRESHOLD: THE EXPERIENCE OF THE GENDER VIOLENCE CAMPAIGN IN LATIN AMERICA AND THE CARIBBEAN

APARNA MEHROTRA[75]

The 20th century may go down in history as the era of breaching frontiers. Within the single decade of the 1960s, human beings reached the moon and began cracking the genetic code. Between insights on interstellar and intermolecular space, scientists also started to build cyberspace—with its own set of new, contested boundaries. Yet our most controversial frontier remains the threshold between "public" and "private" life, the issue that so often stands not only between women and full political participation, but between women and their physical security.

We are very familiar now with the public face of human rights. Massive, excessive violations of human rights such as those in Rwanda, Bosnia, Kosovo and East Timor have brought public human rights and governance issues into sharp focus. However, the time has also come to look directly into the "private" face of human rights: violations of human rights in the personal sphere. If we could change the private face by setting new standards of behaviour, would this not then directly impact on public standards? Are the sustained, increasing and ever-prevalent violations of individual human rights really due only to a crisis of social concern or official policies? Or, are they also due to a crisis of compassion and sensitivity in the home? It is not our heads that have failed us but our hearts. We suffer from a crisis of conscience, a conscience that is founded and molded largely by the education and experience of our homes, in our private compass, the sensitivity of which determines the attitudes and altitudes of our own individual standards for human rights. If all of us, or even most of us, adhered to a high, sensitive private standard, the public standard would surely follow.

Until very recently, governance activities and human rights agendas in particular were focussed in the context of the public sphere alone. The State held the responsibility for good governance by, *inter alia*, providing what were deemed

---

[75] Aparna Mehrotra is currently the Principal Advisor for United Nations Foundation Affairs, UNDP. Ms. Mehrotra was one of the co-founders for the UN Inter-Agency Campaign on Women's Human Rights.

protective measures against possible human rights violations by State authorities and against other crimes. Domestic governance issues, on the other hand—such as human rights violations within the family—were largely relegated to the private domain, where actions were governed by prevailing standards of culture. Thus, crime belonged within the sphere of public governance, culture, within the private sphere; crime was to be addressed, culture was not.

In all countries, statistics indicate that women are safer on the street, unprotected, than they are in their own home. While violence is violence and a victim is a victim everywhere, the victimization seems especially harsh and the violation especially grave when it occurs in the so-called safe haven— the home. There, by definition, it is also accompanied by betrayal, betrayal of the bonds of trust by those who presumably are there to protect one.

Global statistics tell us that the most prevalent and pervasive form of violence and human rights violations occurs against women within their own homes.

At some moment in their lives, over half of all Latin American and Caribbean women have been subjected to an act of violence in their home. Another 33 per cent have been victims of sexual abuse between the ages of 16 and 49, and at least 45 per cent have been threatened, insulted or had their personal possessions destroyed.[76] In some countries, as many as 60 per cent of couples reported suffering from partner abuse.[77] In Colombia, records of the Instituto Nacional de Medicina Legal indicate that one in every 10 victims of sexual abuse is under the age of 4 years.[78] Incredible but true. In Mexico, the Public Defender's Office estimates that on average 82 women are raped every day. And worse still, most often by somebody they know. A majority of rape statistics world-wide follow this pattern.

In the United States, among all female murder victims in 1991, 28 per cent were killed by their husbands or boyfriends.[79] In Alaska in 1990, this figure rises to an astounding 50 per cent.[80]

In some parts of Latin America and the Middle East, a woman may be legally murdered by her husband, father or brother if she is found to be an adulteress.[81] This is obviously a grave violation of human rights, public or private, domestic or otherwise, and should be treated as a criminal act.

In Africa the situation is no different. In South Africa, one woman is killed every six days on account of domestic violence.[82] Similarly, in Rwanda the atrocities have been equally brutal and largely gender-biased.

The UNDP Human Development Report states that no country treats its women as well as its men. A negative differential persists and gender violence in particular has much to do with it. The time to focus on a new paradigm has come, and in recent years an important shift towards this has occurred. State responsibility has been extended to foster a culture of good public governance at large, of which protection against human rights violations in the private sphere are increasingly considered an integral part. It is now further accepted that the overall practice of good governance must evolve from the foundation of good domestic governance, which builds and molds the ideals we expect to be perpetuated in public governance.

What we view happening within the home, therefore, is only the foundation and basis of what we experience in society. Until we create new behaviours and attitudes in private governance, things cannot be expected to change in the public domain, as these two spheres have a symbiotic relationship. Therefore, private governance, i.e., the domestic sphere, takes on extraordinary importance in the creation of individual values and in the creation of the foundation for good public governance. After all, society is a conglomerate of individual attitudes. The contagion effect becomes an interesting phenomenon in molding the values and beliefs of society, because as a few individuals adjust their behaviours, momentum builds and ultimately sways the attitudes of the greater population.

WOMEN'S POLITICAL PARTICIPATION AND GOOD GOVERNANCE: 21ST CENTURY CHALLENGES

[76] ISIS, 1998.
[77] *The World's Women 1995: Trends and Statistics.* New York: United Nations Publications, 1995.
[78] "International Day Against Violence Against Women: Gender-based Violence is an Obstacle to Development", published for United Nations Campaign for Women's Human Rights, 1998.
[79] "Uniform Crime Reports of the US 1991", Federal Bureau of Investigation. Washington, DC: US Department of Justice, 1991, p.18.
[80] "Beyond Beijing: After the Promises of the UN Conference on Women - Who's Doing What to Turn Words into Action?" volume 2, number 1. New York: National Council for Research on Women, 1996, p.29.
[81] United Nations Human Development Report 1995, New York: United Nations, 1995, p. 44.
[82] Mariam Seedat, *End-violence* mail list, September 23, 1999.

Moreover, violence within the home is a largely learned behaviour, similar to other behaviour and values that are learnt and witnessed largely in the home. One of the most important single determinants of violent behaviour as an adult is exposure to it as a child. Witnesses of violence or subjects of it replicate it; they replicate its callousness of conscience and its inherent indignity and violation, transmitting it from one generation to the next, destroying, thereby, not only this but those that follow. Reconstruction and sustenance of a public human rights standard requires that we recognize this and address the private face—violence in the home, violence between partners, violence experienced by children and, the largest component, violence against women—if not for our generation, then for the next. The costs and consequences of violence are not just borne by the direct victim. Rather, the impact is much more far-reaching.

The duplication of behaviour is manifested in both roles; boys largely as the aggressors and girls as the victims. In Canada, it has been found that sons of batterers are 1,000 per cent more likely to beat their own wives.[83] Studies conducted in 1993 in Antigua and Barbados found that 30 per cent of women have experienced violence in their lifetime. Of these, 50 per cent claimed that their mothers had also been battered.[84] An IDB study of Nicaragua shows that the children of abused women were three times more likely to require medical care and that 63 per cent of the children who were exposed to violence in the home had to repeat at least one grade in school. On average these children left school at age nine.[85]

Governance does in fact start within the home. Therefore, concerted focus should be given to the rights and the freedoms experienced within each home. It is well-accepted by psychologists that if certain behavioural patterns are enforced, deeper attitudinal changes eventually follow. Enforcing changed behaviour may be considered the key to altering attitudes. For this to occur the practice of equality and non-violence must first be established within the smaller unit of the home, and later diffused within greater society.

Volumes would be required to cover the legal implications of the interactions of the "public" and "private" spheres. Volumes could also be devoted

to the multiple relationships between law and behaviour on the part of both groups and individuals. This brief paper concentrates on one practical and successful effort to safeguard human dignity: the UN Inter-Agency Campaign to Prevent Violence against Women in Latin America and the Caribbean.

Genesis of the Campaign

In 1993, the World Conference on Human Rights in Vienna held a stirring series of hearings at the Global Tribunal on Violations of Women's Human Rights. There, women from 25 countries testified to a vast range of gender based abuses, from domestic violence to political persecution and violations of economic rights, including war crimes against women and violations of women's bodily integrity. Their testimonies stemmed from situations in polities as diverse as the Netherlands and the Sudan and drew world attention to the stubborn universality of gender-based patterns of coercion.

From the perspective of the United Nations, gender violence represents a violation of that which it holds highest—fundamental values that it considers absolute and on which it cannot accept compromise.

In 1997, under the leadership of both UNIFEM and UNDP, a variety of UN bodies joined forces in a region-wide effort. Latin America and the Caribbean constituted an area ripe for a multi-thrust campaign that could bring together the different strengths of the United Nations system: the United Nations Population Fund (UNFPA), the United Nations Children's Fund (UNICEF), the Joint United Nations Programme Office of the United Nations High Commissioner for Refugees (UNHCR), the Office of the High Commissioner for Human Rights (UNHCHR) and the UN Economic Commission for Latin America and the Caribbean (ECLAC), and UNAIDS.

This became the major area of concern of the UN Women's Human Rights Campaign, the immediate objective of which is to combat gender violence and enforce both the public and the private standard. It is a very concerted and conscious attempt to shift gender violence from a private to a public issue, from an invisible one to a visible one. It must become a public issue with a private face. One African activist said it well: "Violence persists in part because it is hidden. If governments and citizen's groups can expose its magnitude and

[83] *Women: Challenges to the Year 2000*, UN, 1991.
[84] *Violence Against Women: The Hidden Health Burden*, World Bank, 1994.
[85] Inter-American Development Bank Study on Domestic Violence in Chile and Nicaragua, 1998.

character, then ignorance will no longer be an excuse for inaction."[86]

The focus on women was particularly apt because of the fact that the United Nations had appointed a Special Rapporteur on Violence against Women, its Causes and Consequences. The continuing vitality of NGO activity in this area in Latin America and the Caribbean had contributed significantly to making this region the only region in which every country had ratified the 1979 International Convention on the Elimination of Discrimination Against Women (CEDAW).

In 1962, led by the Dominican Republic, the Latin American and Caribbean women's movement established 25 November as a day to denounce violence against women. The movement sought to commemorate the efforts of three Dominican social activists Patricia, Minerva and Maria Teresa Miraval, who were killed on 25 November 1960 under the dictatorship. Thirty-seven years later (December 17, 1999), the General Assembly adopted the resolution formally recognising this day as the International Day to Eliminate Violence Against Women.

Moreover, in 1994, the Organization of American States (OAS) had adopted the Inter-American Convention on the Prevention, Punishment and Eradication of Violence Against Women. For the first time in history, governments were held responsible for acts of violence against women, either "those committed by agents of the State or, indirectly by individuals, and not only for actions, but also for failing to take action."

The Americas had reacted to a markedly mixed record on women's rights—not unlike that of every other region in the world, developed or developing. In Latin America alone, the trends and statistics were alarming. With the restoration of democracy in Argentina, Chile and Uruguay, shocking accounts emerged about the sexual torture of women and girls by the police forces of the earlier military regimes. Even worse, perhaps, were the criminal tendencies and acts explicitly permitted by legitimate regimes: Until 1989 in Ecuador, a husband had the right to force his wife to live with him, whatever his treatment of her. And in Guatemala, Article 114 of the Civil Code, currently under review, grants a husband the right to prohibit his wife from working outside the home, whatever her

WOMEN'S POLITICAL PARTICIPATION AND GOOD GOVERNANCE: 21ST CENTURY CHALLENGES

---

[86] Fatou Thiam, Solidarite, Senegal.

need to achieve the financial independence that would allow her to flee an abusive situation.

Media Action

Given the hidden nature of most violence in the home and its largely ignored consequences and dimensions in the streets as well as other public spaces, the Campaign began by raising general awareness of the problem. A Life Free of Violence: It's Our Right became the slogan of media efforts in 24 countries in English, Portuguese, Spanish and in a number of indigenous languages. In Brazil, it is written on more than a million checks disbursed to federal employees each month, in El Salvador, on police paychecks and consumer utility bills as well. In Ecuador, the slogan and its logo emblazoned a postage stamp and a label affixed to the snacks distributed to school children. Throughout the region, 1300 community and commercial radio stations aired 12 commercial spots produced in four languages by national and regional initiatives. In addition, 11 million television viewers throughout Latin America watched a 30-minute documentary, *Mujeres Protagonistas*, tracing the struggle for women's rights throughout the region, produced by GEMS-TV of Miami.

Though a complete listing of media events would cover several pages, it is worth noting that the campaign's web-site, www.undp.org/rblac/gender, lists related feature articles in English and Spanish, as well as its visual products (buttons, pins, calendars and posters). Most critically, the Campaign has tried to illuminate aspects of gender violence generally neglected by conventional media coverage. These were the manifold health risks and burdens associated with offenses: a range of beatings, malnutrition and clandestine abortion; the physical, psychological and educational consequences for the children of abused mothers, even when they themselves do not directly suffer either physical or verbal violence; gender violence as an obstacle to socio-economic development; and the massive contribution of gender violence to the growing refugee problems of Latin America and the Caribbean.

Legal Reform

A second strategic objective of the Campaign was to sensitize and motivate governments to develop new policies, legislation and practices to prevent violence against women and girls, as well as to repeal laws that encourage it, even indirectly. An illustrative rather than exhaustive list illustrates the directions that legal reform have taken. The Venezuelan Parliament adopted the Law on Violence against Women and the Family, featuring stringent penalties regarding as criminal offences all threats of violence, physical violence, sexual harassment and mental abuse. In Peru, the heads of departments signed an Inter-Ministerial Agreement on Violence against Women. In the context of Haiti's national Plan for Safe Motherhood, the country's Ministry of Health, with support from UNFPA, produced a document on violence against women. In Ecuador, the Municipality of Quito established a Network for the Prevention of Gender Violence with the participation of UNFPA and NGOs. In Brazil representatives of governmental bodies, NGOs and other civil society organizations signed the Community Pact against Violence in November 1998.

Training and Other Capacity-Building Efforts

Since the police on neighbourhood patrol are usually the closest representatives of the law to the home, the Campaign's training on efforts have concentrated initially on reshaping the attitudes and practices of local security authorities. In the Caribbean, a police-training manual and a protocol of cooperation between women's crisis centres and district police stations was developed. The training manual proposes a seven-day course covering existing police policies on domestic violence (including the tendency of police personnel to blame the victim); the legal framework; the effects of sexual assault on victims and society; liaison with non-police agencies; dealing with evidence and the role of forensic and medical personnel; the forms and nature of domestic battering and the sexual abuse of children, along with interviewing techniques to elicit the details of such offenses in view of the shame and other stigma the victim may feel. The course also contains a day-by-day guide for session leaders and handouts for group work.

Similar initiatives have been launched in Brazil, where training manuals have been written and workshops held in the police academics of Rio de Janeiro, Sao Paulo and other major cities. Venezuela has extended police training to the national defense forces, holding seminars on gender-based violence for the National Guard, the Army, the Navy and the

Air Force. As the United Nations Secretary-General Kofi Annan has pointed out, "In recent decades, there has been a dramatic and unacceptable deterioration in the level of adherence to humanitarian norms in crisis situations…. In the past, civilian populations were chiefly indirect victims of fighting between hostile armies. Today they are often the main targets, with women suffering in disproportionate numbers while often also being subjected to atrocities that include organized rape and sexual exploitation. The monitoring and reporting of respect for human rights is a critical responsibility of the international community…"[87]

In Ecuador, UNFPA supported the National Council on Women and the Congressional Special Commission on Women, Children and the Family to present reforms in the Penal Code. In addition, courses on women's human rights have been introduced into the curricula of law faculties, starting with the University of Guayaquil. The UNIFEM Andean Regional Office, together with the national Urban Management Programme of Habitat, launched an annual media contest to award prizes to municipalities that foster women's rights.

Focusing on the extent to which media coverage and its tone conditions the attitudes of authorities to violence against women and penetrates well into the private sphere; in Nicaragua, a country still striving to cope with a legacy of gender abuse fostered by decades of civil strife, the United Nations system has held media seminars for journalists on providing adequate and accurate coverage of family violence.

Alliance-Building

As all the foregoing examples demonstrate, the Campaign has derived much of its success from building political alliances among diverse groups, governmental and non-governmental, including not only civil society organizations but also academic and research institutes and private sector firms. A broad representative sample of partners includes the AMARC Community Radio Stations; ISIS International, based in Chile; the Caribbean Association for Feminist Research and Action (CAFRA); the Colective Radial Feminista and the Manuel Ramos movement of Peru; the Women's

---

[87] Report of the United Nations Secretary-general to the Security Council, *The Causes of Conflict and the Promotion of Durable Peace and sustainable Development in Africa,* United nations, New York, 16 April 1998, pp.11-12.

Communications and Information Centre (CIVAC) of Mexico; the Instituto Social y Politico de la Mujer of Argentina; Cotidiano Mujer of Uruguay; and the Secretariat of Human Rights of the Brazilian Ministry of Justice. Material encouragement to several of these efforts was provided by the UNIFEM Trust Fund in Support of Actions to Eliminate Violence against Women, established in 1996 by the UN General Assembly. Among these activities, a recent municipal initiative has taken place in Honduras for peer education of youth on violence against women in three neighbourhoods with a high incidence of such offenses.[88]

Lessons Learned

The UN Inter-Agency Campaign ran from November 1998 to December 1999. During that period valuable lessons were learned. Some of them are described below.

1. The Human Development Report 1999 states, "Governance does not mean mere government. It means the framework of rules, institutions and established practices that set limits and give incentives for the behaviour of individuals, organizations and firms."[89] In several instances the campaign induced changes in the framework of rules in the form of legislation. More importantly, however, a behaviour and attitudinal change towards violence against women is required. This is only possible when the State works together with civil society, publicly identifying the issue, and clearly addressing the real causes and consequences of acts. A partnership between public and private governance is necessary for effective change to take place.

2. The means must exist for women to break away from domestic violence. In order for this to occur, the silence must be broken in the public sphere. Formal and public messages must be repeatedly broadcast with respect to both the prevalence and the unacceptability of the behaviour. Public fora, legitimate and constructive spaces, safe havens and enforced laws must be created, which encourage and allow women to speak out against violence at the individual and private level.

3. Reporting by governments, as required by all Human Rights Conventions including CEDAW and the Special Rapporteur on Violence against Women, provides an established and legitimate framework for active monitoring. Data collection takes the issue out of the speculative realm and into reality. Facts and figures are a real force to be reckoned with, as they expose reality and reveal the real human costs of gender violence. Thus the need for statistics and data collection cannot be stressed enough; both because it is reflective of an objective need for rational analysis and because it is a cause and consequence of a state of political will. Lack of statistics justifies a lack of policy response, and a lack of policy demonstrates a lack of concern. This has to be rectified; reporting statistics is critical.

The UN Campaign committed itself to the preparation of National Reports on the status of violence against women, to be prepared by the United Nations system, civic and government bodies. The national reports not only contribute through the generation of data but, in addition, they provide for a tangible objective and output around which to galvanize otherwise disperse forces in a relatively unthreatening manner. The reports are not about human rights violations but are compilations of fact and description into a single source. As such they provide a relatively summarized and more user-friendly overview of the issue.

4. The UN name and support adds legitimacy and credibility to the message and to the national campaigns. While the power of the campaign is in its message, when this message receives support and is promoted in association with the UN name, it appears to have greater opportunity to be broadcast, heard and accepted. The prestige and impartiality of the United Nations lend an effectiveness to the delivery and acceptance of public messages; it appears to both place the message more squarely within the human rights framework with which the UN seems to be more clearly identified and imparts a greater dimension of political will and public significance necessary for more serious and effective delivery of the message.

5. Enthusiasm and visible demonstrations of it by leading public and private figures contribute significantly to success of the campaign. The

WOMEN'S POLITICAL PARTICIPATION AND GOOD GOVERNANCE: 21ST CENTURY CHALLENGES

[88] *The Funding Principles and Guidelines*, as well as applications procedures, are available from UNIFEM.
[89] *United Nations Human Development Report 1999*. New York: Oxford University Press, 1999, p. 8.

enthusiasm seems to be a necessary component to ensure persistence and strength needed to prevail despite resistance on several fronts. Projecting an intrinsic sincerity and power on the part of advocates contributes greatly to engaging public and private institutions and actors that would otherwise not partake of the campaign and its message. It becomes fundamental to facilitate the mobilization of civil society at large, broadening the outreach of the campaign. Also, within institutions, demonstrated managerial support on the part of a few individuals perceived to be in "powerful positions" is a significant a catalyst for change.

6. Finally, education on the topic of human rights is the most innocuous entry point for advocacy and change. It is an issue that no government and no organization can be indifferent towards, especially in the growing global community. Governments are realizing their responsibility in promoting basic human rights, and understand the negative repercussions that they must bear when these rights are not upheld.

These considerations argue that domestic violence is to be actively treated as a human rights violation and not as compliance with a culture. It is violation that must be criminalized by national laws and enforced by the judicial system.

Beyond this is individual awareness and commitment. Violence in women's lives will not be eradicated until all members of society refuse to tolerate it. This must include concerted activism by women and men alike. In the end, all collective change is an integration of individual changes. Example is not one way to influence matters; it is the only way.

The significance and importance of such a campaign is not merely to spread awareness to implement tools for punishment and deterrence, but rather to foster change in perception and ideology ... the ultimate goal is PREVENTION and ELIMINATION.

As statistics illustrate, this scourge is perpetuated through an evil cycle. The ultimate goal is to get to the root of the problem by implementing the necessary, if perceived small, changes throughout all the stages of the cycle and by incorporating all actors for the process of change to occur.

As Secretary General Kofi Annan has stated, "women's rights are the responsibility of all humankind; combating all forms of violence against women is the duty of all humankind; and achieving the empowerment of women is the advancement of all humankind."[90]

BIBLIOGRAPHY

Bunch, Charlotte and N. Reilly (1994). *Demanding Accountability: the Global Campaign And Vienna Tribunal for Women's Human Rights,* Centre for Women's Leadership, Rutgers University, New Jersey and UNIFEM, New York.

Carrillo, Roxanna (1992). *Battered Dreams: Violence against Women: an Obstacle to Development,* New York, UNIFEM.

Cook, Blanche Wiesen (1992). *Eleanor Roosevelt, Volume I: 1884-1933,* Penguin Books, New York.

Inter-American Development Bank (1998). Study on Domestic Violence in Chile and Nicaragua, Inter-American Development Bank, Washington. D.C.

National Council for Research on Women (1996). "Beyond Beijing: After the Promises of the UN Conference on Women—Who's Doing What to Turn Words into Action?" volume 2, number 1. New York.

Reineke, Wolfgang H. (1999). "The Other World Wide Web: Global Public Policy Networks", *Foreign Policy,* Number 117, winter, 1999-2000.

United Nations (1991). *Women: Challenges to the Year 2000,* United Nations, New York.

_____ (1995). *The World's Women 1995: Trends and Statistics.* United Nations, New York.

_____ (1997). *Report of the Secretary-General to the Security Council: The Causes of Conflict and Sustainable Development in Africa,* United Nations, New York, 1997.

_____ (1998). *Report of the United Nations Secretary-general to the Security Council, The Causes of Conflict and the Promotion of Durable Peace and Sustainable Development in Africa,* United Nations, New York, 16 April.

United Nations Campaign for Women's Human Rights (1998). "International Day Against Violence Against Women," United Nations, New York.

UNDP (1995) *Human Development Report,* United Nations Development Programme, Oxford University Press, New York and Oxford.

_____ (1999). *Human Development Report.* Oxford University Press, New York and Oxford.

United States of America, Federal Bureau of Investigation (1991). "Gender-based Violence is an Obstacle to Development", published for "Uniform Crime Reports of the US 1991", United States Department of Justice, Washington, D.C.

World Bank. (1994). Violence Against Women: The Hidden Health Burden, World Bank, Washington, DC.

CROSSING THE
GOVERNANCE
PRIVATE
THRESHOLD:
THE EXPERIENCE
OF THE GENDER
VIOLENCE
CAMPAIGN IN
LATIN AMERICA
AND THE
CARIBBEAN

---

[90] Excerpt from the Secretary-General's message for International Women's Day, March 8th 1998

A VOICE OF THEIR OWN: CONCLUSIONS OF THE NEW DELHI MEETING ON WOMEN'S POLITICAL PARTICIPATION: 21ST CENTURY CHALLENGES

PAUL OQUIST[91]

The New Delhi meeting on Women's Political Participation made a number of recommendations that are summarized below:

While constituencies elected in open competition may be preferable and afford more effective influence than reserved seats, affirmative action is required as temporary measure until such time gender equity is attained and sustained.

Women in politics as voters, candidates, elected officials and leaders need to have their political skills enhanced. Formal and informal training are important for these purposes.

Key entry points for women's participation and representation are community-based and non-governmental organisations, local self-governance institutions, local governments, national organisations and movements, the media, academic and research institutions, technological entities, the private sector, the civil service and parliaments.

Strategic gate-keepers that affect participation and representation are local and national political party leaders, media directors and managers, budget formulators, budget approvers and legislative agenda-setters. Gender equity campaigns should prioritise influencing these groups of people.

A critical mass in the form of more widespread participation and of greater numbers in representation is necessary to maintain the momentum of the movement. This constitutes a pre-requisite for faster and more significant advances. Numbers are important. A minimum critical mass is 33 1/3 per cent.

[91] Paul Oquist is Chief of the Governance Unit in the UNDP Country Office in Islamabad, Pakistan.

WOMEN'S POLITICAL PARTICIPATION AND GOOD GOVERNANCE: **21ST CENTURY CHALLENGES**

PART III: CONCLUSIONS

The qualitative impact of both participation and representation also requires a greater critical mass in order to more effectively influence legislative, policy, and budget formulation, implementation, monitoring and evaluation processes. Key areas are decisions on legal gender equity, electoral systems, resource allocation and the institutional transformations required for gender equity through the empowerment of women and other disadvantaged groups.

There is no correlation between the level of economic development and gender equity. There are developing countries with high levels of activity and some major breakthroughs. Of those represented at the conference, India, South Africa, Uganda and Jamaica are cases in point. It must be stressed that in other countries with difficult conditions more modest advances may constitute highly significant, and hard won, advances. These should also be encouraged and recognised.

The objective is not only to achieve gender parity in the long-term but also to sustain and enhance the agenda for short- and medium-term gender equity advances.

A more effective knowledge base is necessary for gender equity in the 21st century. This requires increased capacity in information, analysis and research. Important in this regard is the production of gender disaggregated data, including woman's budgets and gender equity indicators, public policy and action research. Considerable opportunities exist for the translation and circulation of existing materials, as well as their simplification to allow greater access. In the "knowledge century", knowledge should be converted into power for gender equity.

The analysis of national and local government budgets from a gender perspective provides a powerful tool for monitoring the implementation of gender sensitive policy, as well as the lobbying of governments by parliamentarians and civil society. Gender budget initiatives are most effective when they involve a wide range of actors. This requires imaginative strategies to simplify and disseminate information, analysis and lobbying positions that would otherwise intimidate and discourage participation in budgetary debates. The South African learning experience in this area is an important point of reference.

Increased and more systematic formal and informal training is needed to increase the effectiveness of women's political knowledge and skills, as well as their capacity to utilize the emerging gender equity knowledge base. The skill areas involved include the understanding of the formal and informal functioning of politics, fund raising, the media, agenda setting, networking, caucus formation and alliance building, negotiation, lobbying, leadership and elected official-constituent relations, among others. This will make more effective women's roles as voters, candidates, elected officials, and political leaders, from the grass roots to the national and international levels. The training of men is also essential and can facilitate alliance building through gender equity caucuses and other mechanisms.

International, regional, national and local educational, media, advocacy and lobbying campaigns that project the knowledge base, serve as a vehicle for training, address gender equity issues, target power gatekeepers (enumerated earlier), promote alliance building, and disseminate learning experiences. The gender equity movement should be a learning network.

A particularly strategic campaign involves the media image of women, women's participation in politics, and women representatives, as well as their contributions to politics and policy. In many countries prevailing media stereotypes constitute a significant obstacle to the effectiveness of the gender equity movement in general.

Particularly effective campaigns with broad-based alliances can be promoted through the identification of issues that enjoy high levels of consensus. An example is the campaigns against domestic violence that have been initiated in several Latin American countries.

The strengthening of the network of networks of people who can work for gender equity. This includes women and gender sensitive men, grassroots citizens and civil society activists and leaders, candidates, elected officials, political leaders, civil servants, media directors and managers, media workers, academics, religious leaders and other opinion formers, decision makers and action takers.

National and international networks of parliamentarians and local elected officials can form a high leverage network for change processes. Youth,

WOMEN'S
POLITICAL
PARTICIPATION
AND GOOD
GOVERNANCE:
21ST CENTURY
CHALLENGES

indigenous people, blacks and the poor, as well as other disadvantaged people, form groups with interests for social equity. In many countries they are allies or potential allies of the gender equity movement. An expanding universe of a network of networks working toward the same general goals is what constitutes a movement.

National and local caucuses of parliamentarians, women's movement members, and gender-sensitive men who analyse gender information and situations, set common agendas, and work consciously for gender equity can be an effective networking and action mechanism. The Ugandan learning experience provides a valuable point of reference.

UNDP and other UN system agencies, including UNIFEM, should play proactive roles in support of the gender equity movement. This should transcend a facilitating role and additionally include advocacy, media campaign, networking, alliance building and capacity building activities. The latter should entail the promotion of gender disaggregated information, including women's budgets; the interchange of learning experiences between regions and countries;

policy analysis and development support; and educational and training activities. The UNDP Human Development Report is the ideal forum in which to annually project a Gender Equity Index, which should be perfected from year to year. Politically neutral international support is particularly important in countries where prevailing conditions make gender equity advances difficult.

The use of political empowerment to promote the institutional reforms necessary for economic empowerment and poverty reduction. Decentralisation with the devolution of power and resources can facilitate this process. Local political power should strengthen women's national political power, which in turn should create better conditions for wider and more meaningful participation at the local level. The strengthening of this virtuous circle can significantly contribute to the capacity of women to influence political decisions at the local, national and international levels, as well as improve the quality of their lives and those of other disadvantaged groups. Political power should be transformed into economic power, which further enhance political power.

A VOICE OF
THEIR OWN:
CONCLUSIONS
OF THE NEW
DELHI MEETING
ON WOMEN'S
POLITICAL
PARTICIPATION:
21ST CENTURY
CHALLENGES

CHAPTER 10

THINK GLOBALLY, ELECT LOCALLY?

LINA HAMADEH-BANERJEE

"Think globally, act locally" became the slogan of the world-wide environmental movement as preparations began for the 1992 United Nations Conference on Environment and Development, better known by its abbreviated name: the Earth Summit. The example of women elected to the highest political offices of their countries has inspired a great number of other women to run for high office in a significant demonstration of the "trickle-down" effect. However, economic experience globally has tended to indicate that this kind of downward movement stops short of the poor. In the political realm, it is by and large elite women who have triumphed in the gender struggle for office. What can be said for a movement that begins at the bottom?

The need to share experiences has prompted the entry of village activities into global learning networks, particularly for women. Electronic information technology has accelerated this process immensely. The experience of the Indian Panchayati raj experiment has consequently penetrated both international forums and even villages.

The Implications of the Indian Experiment

The Panchayati raj experiment, examined in Chapter 5 of this collection, stimulated considerable discussion at the meeting on Women's Participation: 21st Century Challenges. The exchange centred on three fundamental questions:

> Does political participation at the grassroots level provide a testing ground for politicians to move from local to national leadership?
>
> Does this apply to women?
>
> Can quota systems at the local level—33 1/3 per cent in India—be up-scaled to the national level?

The Panchayati raj experiment is too new to provide conclusive answers even in India. However, together with comparable efforts elsewhere in the world, a variety of interesting observations arose.

As a 1997 United Nations periodical remarked:

> *"Women's participation in local politics has long been viewed as an extension of women's traditional involvement in household management. This idea*

WOMEN'S
POLITICAL
PARTICIPATION
AND GOOD
GOVERNANCE:
**21ST CENTURY
CHALLENGES**

can be used either to devalue or to promote efforts to increase women's numbers in local government, where their political activity has so far been most marked. However, current trends towards the devolution of power may make holding local office a far more powerful and prestigious occupation than it has been up to the present. Because so many women still shoulder disproportionate responsibilities for household management and therefore cannot leave home for remote capitals, devolution provides a significant means of making their voices heard nationally."[92]

As many participants in the UNDP meeting on women's political participation agreed, the Indian experiment of introducing local democracy into a feudal society showed mixed results. The most dramatic criticism was that the women elected to the village Panchayati were perceived as puppets of their male family members. A multiplicity of obstacles arose not only from proxy politics, but from caste and class as well. As the authors of Chapter 5 pointed out, the Constitutional amendment that set the experiment in motion established caste as well as gender quotas and did not adequately reflect the fact that women make up at least half the population of the scheduled castes and tribes.[93] In addition, observers have drawn a distinction between "people's politics" and "party politics".

Nonetheless, approximately one million women throughout India became political decision makers for the first time. In West Bengal, the fact that 70 per cent of the women elected to the village Panchayati were landless and lower-caste led to a breakdown of landowners' control over the political process. In Karnataka and Rajasthan, women transformed local political agendas. Throughout the country, NGOs representing 5.2 million slum-dwellers mobilized their women members to benefit from the new quota system by standing for local council seats. Moreover, as participants observed, the dichotomy between "people's" and "party" politics is false. Women must impact on party politics and bring the experiences of grassroots democracy to party politics—as they have done in a number of countries, both industrialised and developing, ranging from Sweden to Uganda.

However, women's political participation cannot be viewed in isolation from political institutions. In India, as in other countries, when women became visibly active in local government, they were unrealistically expected to solve mainstream political problems, such as feudalism, corruption, criminal activity and caste and class divisions, even (and perhaps especially) where authorities had taken no action to empower these new, often ill-educated council members with legal literacy and other training for political life.

Whatever the case, the UNDP meeting participants urged, opportunities should be seized, since local politics can provide opportunities for a non-hierarchical system. In addition, the dissemination of local information can be used to support transparency and accountability and thereby counter corruption. All in all, the Panchayati raj experiment so far indicated significant linkages between strong civil society movements, increased political participation by women, and improved community dialogue.

Experience in Other Countries

Looking as far from India as Madagascar and Costa Rica, participants made a number of observations. In Madagascar, structural barriers to women's participation emerge along rural/urban lines, despite the fact that Malagasy society is matrilineal and, in some areas, matriarchal. In the countryside, poor families tend to sacrifice their daughters' education to that of their sons. On the other hand, urban women have access to high positions; the country's second largest city has a woman mayor and four of Madagascar's 12 cabinet ministers are women. Elsewhere in Africa, the Association of Local Authorities in Botswana conducted a workshop for strengthening the capacities of women councilors.

In Latin America, where economic globalisation has doubled extreme poverty and exacerbated social dislocations, grassroots democracy seems to be a channel for enhancing the pace of human development. Increasing women's political participation also appears to be essential. In Costa Rica, of 5071 municipal administrators, only 196 are women—despite government promises to enlarge women's participation to 40 per cent at the ministerial level and to increase their numbers in other government institutions. In 1995, the Association of Ecuadorian Municipalities and the country's Association of Women Municipal Elected Officials established a support structure for women mayors and councilors. And the Andean Division of the International Union

WOMEN'S POLITICAL PARTICIPATION AND GOOD GOVERNANCE: 21ST CENTURY CHALLENGES

[92] "Women in Decision-Making", *Women 2000*, United Nations, NY, October 1997.
[93] An analogous criticism emerged in the early years of the USA experience of affirmative action in hiring and school admissions during the 1960s. Universities and private enterprises were accused of selecting African-American women at the expense of African-American men so as to be able to fill two quota requirements with one individual.

of Local Authorities (IULA) has issued papers on integrating gender perspectives in municipal development plans, focusing on gender budgeting in development planning, health, education, and environment.

In many countries that achieved political independence during the 20th century and earlier, women fought side by side with men during the struggle for national sovereignty, but were soon forgotten by their male leaders. Moreover, after independence, these leaders emphasized national issues at the expense of local questions and thus weakened the powers of local governments. In most developing countries today, formal structures at the national level tend to penetrate informal, often local structures and thereby perpetuate national political power patterns.

The experience of Palestinian women adds another aspect to this world-wide picture. Although their participation in the liberation process had been widely and publicly acknowledged, the Women's National Machinery found during the first national elections that the majority of the youth did not vote for women. By contrast, professional men did, challenging the general view that the young people are more liberal than their elders. Consequently, the women's movement began establishing coalitions between various political groups to work with the youth population over (some 40 per cent of the people of both Gaza and the West Bank). They also started to training women for local government activity.

IULA Action World-wide

Founded 1n 1913, headquartered in Amsterdam, and representing local governments and/or authorities and their associations in some 100 countries, IULA began promoting gender equality in the 1990s. Its Women in Local Government Task Force, headed by the Swedish Association of Local Authorities, established a network for sharing initiatives and best practices that covers the multiple roles of local authorities as primary planners, providers of services—notably for social welfare—and employers. Its 1998 policy paper not only set out common obstacles to women's participation in local government, but contained overviews and recommendations for seven regions. The subsequent World-wide Declaration on Women in Local Government committed IULA members to strengthen their efforts to reach gender parity in decision-making bodies at all levels.

Grassroots Organisations

Although women's participation in local government decision-making bodies remains low world-wide, their participation in grassroots organisations has increased. As noted in the chapter of this collection on Women's Agency for Government, women's ambivalence about formal political structures, repeatedly manifest at the New Delhi meeting, stems in part from unwillingness to become involved in corruption and traditional ethnic and class disputes. By contrast, their work in grassroots organisations has given them opportunities for activities in different modalities, in environments that encourage team-work,[94] and in situations where the outcomes of their efforts are visible. Participants also observed that women not only feel comfortable working in organisations with other women, but that they are reluctant to join organisations that perpetuate patriarchal structures, governmental or non-governmental. At the same time, the participants remarked that the enormous growth of grassroots organisations stems in large measure from dissatis-faction with the state as a provider of services.

In India, Swayam Shikshan Prog (SSP) in Mumbai has organised women's collectives to change community ownership and to increase community contributions and tax collection. They monitor the functioning of basic services in such areas as physical infrastructure, health care, and education. These women, like their counterparts throughout the country, tend to demand greater accountability from local elected representatives.

In Venezuela, however, women community leaders report that their presence is not felt at the municipal level, that this blunts the effectiveness of their organisations, and that it results in barring poor women from political opportunities available to elite and middle class women, largely the former.

Building the capacity of grassroots organisations for partnerships with local governments appears critical to dialogue between them. The SSP model is three-pronged: participation in civic forums; involvement in planning and managing services; and undertaking gender and community audits in tandem with designing alternative approaches.

---

[94] The point has been made by many groups elsewhere. Women's leadership styles, in contrast to those of men, appear to encompass maintaining a complex network of relationships within as well as outside their organisations, scheduling time for the sharing of information and a strong awareness of the value of consensus and agreement. These attributes have been ascribed to women's early training world-wide in fostering social relationships. For a birds'-eye view of the subject, see the October 1997 issue of *Women 2000*.

THINK GLOBALLY, ELECT LOCALLY?

Professional Women's Organisations

At the First World Conference on Women in 1975, one elite professional woman remarked that she had never found herself in a situation where "the major sanitation facility [was] the afternoon vulture". Since that time, most feminist professionals have tried increasingly to bridge the socio-economic gap. In India, there is an association of elected women officials. In Egypt, the feminist organisation *Huda* devotes itself to raising the political self-awareness of their countrywomen and lobbying for increasing women's representation through the electoral process. In Russia, women journalists have united to sensitize their compatriots, male and female, to gender issues, and have founded an international magazine (in Russian) to enhance educational dialogue on these questions. The Super Coalition on Women, Homes and Community—commonly called the Hairou Commission because of its advocacy at the NGO Forums of both the Beijing and the Habitat II[95] Conferences—brings professional and grassroots women together on human settlements questions, both urban and rural, and strives to build alliances with other CSOs, CBOs, government at all levels and the private sector. All these organisations, as well as many more, take advantage of information technology wherever possible.

Conclusions of the New Delhi Working Group on Dialogue Between Different Actors in Local Governance

A working group convened to discuss this subject further at the UNDP meeting on Women's Political Participation: 21st Century Challenges. It highlighted the following lessons:

> Although dialogue and co-operation between NGOs and local governments can relieve some problems, it is not identical to opening windows of opportunity for collaborative interventions and creative ways to solve development problems.

> Dialogues are processes of engagement and do not necessarily imply consensual working relationships.

> NGO involvement in development programmes and projects can fill a vacuum where local government does not service supply adequately.

Consultation between local authorities, the private sector and NGOs prior to undertaking projects is essential to ensuring a good communication process and thereby minimizing duplication of activities and improving their collective impact.

The role of the media in gender sensitization activities at the local level is critical; the media should assume a more proactive role.

So far, legislation has been lagging in clarifying the different roles and functions of national and international NGOs and the extent of their autonomy.

The spectrum of CSO activities has broadened to highlight the role of women's movements in different countries with regard to collaborative efforts and the use of data-based research.

Looking Forward and Back

Concluding this chapter, it seems apt to echo the Introduction to the compilation of plenary speeches from the NGO Forum of the Fourth World Conference on Women:

> *"… with the expansion of transnational activity not subject to the laws of nations, the responsibility of governments to ensure justice, economic and otherwise, and to protect people from policies that threaten their livelihoods or their very lives has taken on new urgency. The strategies that women have used and might use to engage and confront the private sector, state and international organisations are critical for the future."*[96]

If this is true in the NGO realm, it may apply to that of formal political office as well. And if so, the bottom—the local—seems as good a point as any other for the world-wide movement for gender equality.

BIBLIOGRAPHY
Friedlander, Eva, ed. (1996). *Look at the World Through Women's Eyes: Plenary Speeches from the NGO Forum on Women: Beijing '95,* New York.
International Union of Local Authorities (1998). *Women in Local Government,* World Executive Committee of IULA, Helsinki, June.
United Nations (1997). "Women in Decision-Making", *Women 2000,* New York, United Nations, October .

WOMEN'S
POLITICAL
PARTICIPATION
AND GOOD
GOVERNANCE:
21ST CENTURY
CHALLENGES

---

[95] Also known as the United Nations Second Conference on Human Settlements, held in Istanbul in June 1996.
[96] Eva Friedlander, editor, *Look at the World Through Women's Eyes: Plenary Speeches from the NGO Forum on Women: Beijing '95,* New York, 1996

BUDGETS: THE POLITICAL BOTTOM LINE

LINA HAMADEH-BANERJEE

All budgets are about politics. All politics are ultimately about who controls budgets.

The budget is the ultimate tool for governments in implementing their policies. It has to be interpreted from the viewpoint of the differing positions of men and women in the economy. Whatever they may be, government policies translate into allocations that have different impacts for women and for men. Budgets look neutral with regard to gender. The people who develop them may think they are neutral. The differentials become manifest largely at the operational level—when the allocations are translated into deliveries.

Recent years have witnessed a growing awareness of the gender blindness of national budgets. This has increasingly led feminist economists and political economy specialists to draw attention to the gender aspects of macroeconomics that shape national budgets. Recent years have also witnessed progress in the operationalization of gender-focused analytical research concurrent with collective efforts in integrating gender into national budgetary policies and procedures. The most advanced and well-known initiative in the developing countries has been the South African Women's Budget.

Given the uniqueness of the South African experience, UNDP commissioned a paper on the subject for its 1999 New Delhi meeting on Women's Political Participation: 21st Century Challenges. It was directed in large measure to parliamentarians and senior government officials whose professional work includes the preparation, analysis and endorsement of national and sectoral budgets. Moreover, UNDP also aimed at creating an awareness of the critical advocacy role of civil society for advancing the goal of mainstreaming gender concerns into national budgets. Below is a summary of the session discussion.

Sharing Experience

South Africa

The rationale behind the South African Women's Budget is its adoption of comprehensive approach to the whole government budget in terms of how allocations are divided among women and men, and girls and boys. The strong message of this budget exercise was the prioritisation of scarce resources.

The women's budget approached these priorities using a needs-based approach and in that context priorities are determined on the basis of those who need it most regardless to whether they are men or women, boys or girls. With this point of departure, the Women's Budget examines priorities within the following parameters: (a) gender-specific targeted projects, (b) expenditure on government employees, and in particular, the gender distribution of public servants at the decision-making level, including the presence of women in important delivery positions such as at the policy making level for monitoring violence, and (c) examining the bulk of budgetary allocation to determine who actually receives funds allocated in such areas as education and, agriculture and who benefits, both directly and indirectly.

The Women's Budget examines not only expenditure on social services, but the gender implications of revenue generation, such as the impact of taxes on women and the poor. Because women tend to earn less income than men, a regressive taxation system would leads to working women's paying a larger portion of their income than men, since the portion of their tax proportion is a large part of smaller income. The Women's Budget also examines donor-funded activities to determine their gender advocacy role and their impact on government funded activities. The fact that donor-funded activities favour gender-sensitive programmes may trigger negative effects: gender-related activities may end up not being covered by government funds because of the expectation that donor funding will cover them.

The three-tier process of the exercise expands the analytical process from the national budget (encompassing external technical co-operation budgetary allocations) to a wider view of the economy that includes the household. In this third tier, it focuses on two levels: the care economy and the reproductive economy operate. In this case it examines what assistance is provided by the state to the reproductive economy, such as the provision of childcare, and to the caring economy in the form of medical insurance.

The experience of the Women's Budget n South Africa is more than a collection of sectoral analyses. It is about operationalising the 1993 Women's Charter and translating its stipulations into a concrete and prioritised order, initially concentrating on 6 sectors, then gradually expanding it to cover other sectors. It is also about a unique strategic alliance development and collaboration among different groups with common interests: parliamentarians, civil servants, NGOs, academics, etc. and a unique division of labour among these different allies. The civil servants provided the data, the non-governmental organisation carried out operational advocacy-focused research and sharpened the advocacy arguments, and parliamentarians lobbied. The result was a synergy between women in government, parliamentarians and non-governmental organisations in creating external as well as internal lobby for change. Internally its influence has been profound, impacting on the Ministry of Finance publishing its own "women's budget". Externally, it has had significant effects elsewhere in East Africa: similar initiatives were started in Mozambique, Tanzania and Uganda.

Uganda

Ugandan women activists had been trying to increase the number of women participating in politics since 1985. Significant numbers of women in politics were reached in 1995, at which time the activists among them raised questions as to the impact of women in changing the political agenda and transforming the institutions of governance. There was also a clear sense of frustration that women parliamentarians could not factor gender issues into the budget. Seeking a solution to this frustration, women leaders adopted a problem-solving approach to cope with the many obstacles they faced.

The first problem they encountered was the technical language used in budget formulation and documentation and the ensuing floor discussion. It then became clear to women parliamentarians that they had to learn and practice the use of the distinct language of economists and budget planners. Second, they set in motion a process of learning to understand how budget priorities are set, allocations determined and funds spent. Third, women parliamentarians wanted to improve the efficiency of the delivery of government services by learning from the behaviour of non-governmental organisations, which tend to spend less than governments and to reduce their costs. Their next step was making a difference in determining the budgetary priorities.

In achieving their objectives, they committed themselves to understanding the macro-economic framework and how it is determined. In this learning process, they found that the decision-making for the budgetary framework involved a few powerful individuals from different institutions, namely: the

International Monetary Fund (headquarters and country representative), the World Bank's headquarters and country representative, the Ministry of Finance, Ministry of Planning, the Treasury, the President and a handful of partners. In essence, the in-country decision-making process involved only 6 to 8 people.

Concerned with this anti-democratic process in budget formulation, the Ugandan women parliamentarians determined to learn more and decided to do so in collaboration with representatives of women, youth, and the disabled who were co-members of a common caucus. Together, these representatives ran workshops to master the relationship between the macroeconomic framework and the budgetary framework. In so doing, they learned that there was usually only a 5 per cent variation from the current year to the next and, that therefore in most cases, no fresh evaluation of priorities was carried out. The biases and prejudices contained in the budget were consequently perpetuated from year to year.

Determined to reform the budget process and bolstered by the training in budget analysis, members of the Caucus told the bureaucrats that since the budget is a political instrument, they as parliamentarians needed to take part in all processes involved in its formulation, presentation, adoption and implementation. This constituted the beginning of a concerted effort to reform the budgetary process that soon evolved into informing the public about the timing and content of the budget process.

Simultaneously, with external support from South Africa, and internal support from civil servants (within different governmental sectors who would provide gender disaggregated information required for analysis), economists, local government officials and civil society, skill training was provided in gender awareness, advocacy and gender analysis—initially focusing on the areas of health, education and agriculture and eventually reaching every sector.

Following this, the women parliamentarians convened a conference on women in politics, attended by more than 100 women, to mobilize political support and develop alliances and partnership built on information-sharing. One lesson of this experience was the necessity of creating pressure on government officials with specific reference to the budget. First, however, pressure groups needed to understand the language used in government documents and then to make it public in simplified form—such as the fact that government subsidies for petrol were higher than those for kerosene and that the beneficiaries of government subsidies for petrol were therefore the rich, while the vast majority of Uganda's population, the poor, did not benefit equitably from the kerosene subsidy. A year later, the government increased its subsidies for kerosene.

Jamaica

The national budget of Jamaica has a unique multi-pronged approach in addressing gender-differentiated needs of women and men in its allocations because it made provisions for special funds that targeted different segments of society. Many of these special funds, complementary in nature, provide opportunities through programmes that tend to impact positively on women, notably the Social Development Fund, which focuses on alleviating poverty and thereby ultimately reaches poor women.

In addition, Jamaica's Poverty Alleviation Programme specifically targets pregnant and lactating women in poverty-stricken households. While its primary targets are women in female-headed households, it also targets women in male-headed households, since in Jamaica, many male-headed households have women as their primary earners. Over and above this, through its Skills 2000 Programme, the Jamaican government devotes considerable attention to strengthening its human capital by aiming to lift women's conditions associated with minimum wage income skills development.

At another level, the Social Investment Fund is geared towards addressing the public aspects of poverty such as funding mapping exercises of poverty pockets throughout the country. Another fund, the Fund for Women provides for women-specific sectoral programmes through allocations earmarked for each ministry. A similar modality is used for the Local Development Fund, which is made available to all members of Parliament to assist them in meeting the needs of their constituencies without having to defer to ministries or other agencies.

The Social and Economic Support Fund is yet another fund that is also accessible to all members

**BUDGETS:
THE POLITICAL
BOTTOM LINE**

of parliament; it has a specific provision that requests for funding should indicate how women will benefit directly or indirectly. In addition, the Micro-investment Development Agency provides an avenue for entrepreneurship by offering micro funding for women.

Another feature unique to the Jamaican budget process is the tradition of women members of parliament meeting with the Minister of Finance on the gender-related content of the budget. In addition, each Minister is given an indicative budget with a ceiling. With support from teams who contribute to the prioritization of the allotments, the Ministers decide on their sectoral gender-focused priorities.

The consultation process includes holding meetings with inter-agency and inter-ministry groups that focus on gender issues. This consultative network approach facilitates each Ministry's budget endorsement at the time when all women representatives, including representatives from the Back Benches, meet with the Minister of Finance to ensure that women's needs are well taken into consideration. Finally, at the time the Finance Committee meets on the budget, it is also expected to pass through another round of screening to determine the impact of the budget on women.

Beyond these mechanisms, as the result of the 1996 constitutional reform, a 1997 Act of Parliament established a Gender and Social Equity Commission, with a mission to promote gender and social equity through gender-sensitive approaches to development. It functions as a quasi-judicial body that covers advisory, monitoring, evaluation, information, communication and implementation services. Its objective is to engender the national industrial policy so as to secure economic growth. The Commission also reviews programmes from gender perspective to guarantee women equal access and full participation in all structures, so that social equity and gender equity become recognized as basic requirements for human development.

WOMEN'S
POLITICAL
PARTICIPATION
AND GOOD
GOVERNANCE:
21ST CENTURY
CHALLENGES

Although all the above have made tremendous headway in changing the budget, women still suffer economically. There remains a need for continuous work at the macroeconomic level to ensure that the interests of men and women are reflected equally.

India

Although India is one of the few countries with a woman Deputy Chairperson of the House, women occupy only 8.9 per cent of its seats: 19 out of 220.[97] Nevertheless, during the budget hearings, women parliamentarians succeeded in tabling an agenda item on women's needs that resulted in an agreement to devote 30 per cent of development projects to women. Similarly, at the civil society level, some progress was achieved when a group of economists involved in the Annual Economic Survey of India presented an alternative survey and projections. This in itself was an important exercise because it contributed to mass awareness of gender issues.

Other positive models where the gender lens was successful have been at the local level of the Panchayati raj where the per centage of women elected is mandated at 33 per cent. The most positive example was in the southern state of Kerala, where state authorities adopted a "people's planning process" through which all villagers in Kerala come together on certain days to present their planning priorities to the local government. Initially, only 10 per cent of these groups were women. With time, this grew to over 40 per cent. Professional planners have been drawn to learn from this model because its approach appears to have two significant advantages: it is far more holistic than other planning at the local level and certainly closer to the interests of people at the grassroots level.

Latin America

The Latin American experience has sensitized budgeting to gender concerns at the level of the municipality. A 1994 meeting convened under the auspices of the International Union for Local Authorities (IULA) in Bolivia resulted in a co-operative effort among the Latin American members of the Association to document the integration of gender perspectives into development plans of municipalities. The work focused on four sectors: health, education, environment and urban planning. These documents have since been published in Spanish by CELCADER, the IULA sub-regional division in Quito, Ecuador, under the title "How to Apply Gender Perspective in the Budget for Development Planning, Health, Education and Environment."

---

[97] Data cited by Inter-Parliamentary Union web site.

UNDP as an Example of Gender Budgeting in Multilateral Institutions

Participants in the New Delhi meeting also expressed interest in the UNDP history of gender-sensitive planning. Although the Programme had specified "women in development" as a budget item as early as 1975, no major change took place until 1990, when the Executive Board directed the UNDP Administrator to posit gender as one of the organisation's six priorities. Shortly thereafter, work began on the *Human Development Report 1995*, devoted to gender, which constituted a major UNDP contribution to the Fourth World Conference on Women, held in Beijing a few months after this influential yearly publication was issued.

The *Human Development Report 1995* contained two significant new indicators. The first, the Gender-related Development Index (GDI), measures the inequalities between men and women in all countries of the world with a focus on expanding capabilities. The second, the Gender Empowerment Measure (GEM) examines the extent to which men and women are able to participate actively in economic and political life, particularly at the decision-making level.

With the introduction of these two indicators, UNDP began to address formally the earmarking of funds for women within its programme budget. In 1996, the Administrator of UNDP issued a directive on gender equality and the advancement of women to all staff. That directive promulgated that 20 per cent of the regular, ten per cent of the global and 15 per cent of the country programmes be devoted to gender issues. Since that time, two pilot tracking exercises have monitored these allocations.

The Administrator also addressed the question of critical mass in human resources by a policy on gender balance in management, setting the goal of reaching a 40 per cent for women in management positions and within the overall UNDP workforce by the year 2001. Accordingly, senior managers report regularly to the Administrator on progress towards this target.

Additional opportunities for increasing allocations more equitably along gender lines often occur during periods of transition or reform, whether nationally or internationally. For example, the United Nations reform process has placed greater emphasis on the co-ordination of all the development efforts of the entire system at the country level, within the framework of the United Nations Resident Coordinator for Development Activities. In this context, inter-agency gender committees have been formed at the country level. One achievement in India, cited by the UN Resident Coordinator, was that at the government's request, gender had been selected as a major area of concentration in the United Nations Development Activities Framework.

Lessons Learned

Organisational aspects

Participants manifested overwhelming interest in the South African initiative, which came to fruition through the collaborative efforts of women parliamentarians and activists from the NGO community to capture a significant part of the national wave for change inherent in the post-Apartheid era. Two NGOs were at the centre of this initiative, but the real strength came from the division of labour assigned among individuals and groups. Sectoral NGO specialists and other academics carried out the research. A "reference group" was assigned for each phase. Its membership included at least one insider from the civil service, one advocacy expert, one analyst, and one trainer experienced in team building. The Initiative also produced a book entitled Money Matters, which was used for training. The group also decided to focus on the three-year medium-term framework, since this duration would provide adequate time for interventions. In addition, the group realised that while Parliament could give broad direction, the bureaucrats were responsible for developing the budget, presenting it and implementing it. Consequently, an alliance among them is critical for success.

Empowering Women to Have a Voice in the Budget

Although women frequently determine their household budgets, their voices are barely heard with regard to national budgets. This includes women in legislatures. Participants therefore raised questions on empowering women in and out of office in budgetary affairs. Clearly, as newcomers to the budgetary process, women legislators and other women politicians need support internally and externally and may also require training in macroeconomics. Conversely, the planners who are involved in budget formulation, analysis and implementation need supplementary training in gender budgeting to begin understanding how budgets impact half the population of their countries.

The role of civil society in this process is also critical, not only in contributing to policy analysis, but in providing external pressure. This, in turn, requires the strengthening of skills in lobbying and in combining strategy and tactics in advocacy work.

In addition to training, the process of accessing information and knowledge is extremely important. Since information sources are normally scattered, it is essential to learn what information maybe required for the budget preparation and analysis, where the materials may be found and how they can be accessed, and, finally who are the key persons and institutions for policy and data analysis willing to collaborate. In this connection, the Institute of Development Studies of the University of Sussex, UK, with funding from the Swedish International Development Agency, prepared a publication on resource materials on budgets currently available on its web site (http://www.ids.ac.uk/bridge). In addition to this, there now exists a manual on the basics of gender-sensitive budgeting in English.[98] Its translation into other languages would be useful for women all over the world.

Tactics

South Africa's political change created a fluidity that allowed for co-operation and synergy among all governance partners. An interesting modality adopted by the Budget Initiative group was to piggyback their work onto the agendas of other groups, such as one working on improving transparency measures. This collaborative effort added gender as a supplementary dimension and thereby added value to the efforts of other parties. Again, the importance of women's alliance building comes to the fore.

[98] Debbie Budlender and Rhonda Sharp with Kerri Allen (1998): *How to do a gender-sensitive budget analysis: Contemporary research and practice*, Australian Agency for International Development, Canberra, Australia and Commonwealth Secretariat, London, United Kingdom. It is distributed by the Commonwealth Secretariat, Marlborough House, Pall Mall, London SW1Y 5HX, Fax (44) 0171 9300 827.

Entry Points for Participation in the Budget Process

The importance of seizing windows for gender-related interventions during the budget preparatory process cannot be underestimated. First, policy analysis makes a difference when it is substantiated by data.

Second, public opinion can act as an indicator for measurement of policy congruence and the effectiveness of government response to priorities. Public opinion surveys can serve as objective feedback instruments to inform policy makers. Public opinion can also act as a major force for accountability in government, creating expectations that impel governments to provide information on the implementation of their budgets. In Uganda, government ministries are required to publish actual disbursements to local authorities, including the checks issued.

Third, in the context of results-oriented implementation, entry points can be found by analyzing functions in relation to bureaucratic structures so as to identify deficiencies in effectiveness, capacity, efficiency, and institutional leakages. This is fundamentally a matter of control and oversight at all levels of bureaucracy, particularly for preventing both petty and grand corruption.

Fourth, oversight by NGOs and think tanks can create pressure on legislatures to fulfil the vigorous oversight roles that are rightly theirs vis-à-vis the executive branch and to actually monitor policy impact. This is a constant struggle in all democracies.

Fifth, Independent judicial oversight is also critical. Other processes can contribute to its effectiveness, namely the functions of the General Auditor or policy auditor, which can be expanded to carry out environmental audits, gender audits and social audits.

Finally, in the context of accountability, collaboration between the government as provider of information and civil society role as a watchdog can provide a point of intervention and feedback. The use of indicators such as those developed by the UNDP Human Development Reports with respect to gender, poverty, social development and governance can serve as guidelines and points of leverage, as well frames of reference for comparison at international and sub-national levels.

ANNEXES

NOTE OF APPRECIATION

This report is the product of all those participants who shared their views, experiences, insights and ideas that vibrate in the text of this report. The United Nations Development Programme wishes to extend its appreciation for their valuable participation.

Hon. Rahat Atchylova, Deputy of the Legislative Assembly
Chairman of the Commission on Education, Youth, Women and Family Issues of
  Legislative Assembly of Kyrgystan Parliament, Biskek, Kyrgyzstan

Ms. Bisi Adeleye-Fayemi, Akina Mama wa Africa
Wesley House, 4 Wild Court, Holborn, London WC2B4AU, United Kingdom

Ms. Amat al-Alim al-Souswa, Deputy Minister of Information and Chairperson
  of Women's National Committee
P.O. Box 11844, Sanaa, Yemen

Ms. Begum Hashmat Ara, Assistant Director Deputy of Women's Affairs
Ministry of Women and Children Affairs, Dhaka, Bangladesh

Ms. Nadezhda Azgikhina, Association of Women Journalists
Moscow, Russian Republic, Lesnaia 63/43#151, Moscow 103055, Russia

Ms. Sally Baden, Institute of Development Studies
Sussex University, Brighton, Sussex, United Kingdom

Ms. Farzana Bari, Acting Director, Center for Women's Studies
Quaid-I-Azam University, Islamabad, Pakistan

Ms. Elena Borsatti, Consultant, United National Development Programme
P.O. Box 3059, 55 Lodi Estate, New Delhi 110 003, India

Dr. Angela Briceño, Director of Social Development
Ministry of Labour and the Family
Torre Oeste DE Parque Central, Piso 41, Caracas, Venezuela

Ms. Debbie Budlender, Community Agency for Social Equity
20 Alfred St. Observatory, Cape, 7925, South Africa

Ms. Neera Burra, Assistant Resident Representative
United Nations Development Programme
P.O. Box 3059, 55 Lodi Estate, New Delhi 110 003, India

WOMEN'S
POLITICAL
PARTICIPATION
AND GOOD
GOVERNANCE:
21ST CENTURY
CHALLENGES

Hon. Winnie Byanyima, Member of Parliament
    Forum for Women in Democracy
8th Floor, Embassy House
Parliament Avenue, P.O. Box 7176
Kampala, Uganda

Ms. Mithulina Chatterjee, Programme Assistant
Community Mobilisation Division
United Nations Development Programme
P.O. Box 3059, 55 Lodi Estate
New Delhi 110 003, India

Mr. Shabbir Cheema, Director
Management Development
    and Governance Division
Bureau for Development Policy
United Nations Development Programme
One United Nations Plaza
New York, NY 10017, USA

Hon. Jane Chikwata, Deputy Minister
Ministry for Community Development
    and Social Services
PIB W252, Lusaka, Zambia

Mr. Richard Conroy, Senior Deputy
    Resident Representative
United Nations Development Programme
P.O. Box 3059, 55 Lodi Estate
New Delhi 110 003, India

Ms. Andra Freiberg, UNDAF Support Officer
United Nations Development Programme
P.O. Box 3059, 55 Lodi Estate
New Delhi 110003, India

Ms. Prema Gopalan
Society for Promotion of Area
    Resource Centres (SPARC)
Byculla Area Resource Centre
Meghraj Sethi Marg, Municipal Dispensary, Byculla
Mumbai 400 008, India

Ms. Lina Hamadeh-Banerjee
Senior Programme Advisor
Management Development and
    Governance Division
Bureau for Development Policy
United Nations Development Programme
One United Nations Plaza
New York, NY 10017, USA

Dr. Najma Haptulla
Deputy Chairperson of Rajya Sabha Parliament

House and UNDP Distinguished Human
Development Ambassador and Vice President
of the Executive Committee of Inter-
Parliament Union Executive Committee
New Delhi, India

Dr. Saad Eddin Ibrahim
Chairperson, Ibu Khaldoun Cenrre
P.O.Box No. 13, 17 Street No12
El Mokattem,Cairo, Egypt

Dr. Devaki Jain
Singamma Sreenivasan Foundation
'Tharanga', 10th Cross, Rajmahal Vilas Extension
Bangalore 560 080, India

Ms. Chandni Joshi, Regional Advisor
UNIFEM
P.O. Box No. 3059, 55 Lodi Estate
New Delhi 110003, India

Ms. Zahira Kamal, Geneal Director
Directorate of Gender Planning and
    Development Ministry of Planning
    and International Cooperation
The Palestinian Authority
El-Ram, West Bank, Palestine

Dr. Azza Karam
Middle East Program Director
The Queens University of Belfast
Belfast, Northern Ireland, United Kingdom

Mr. Brinda Karat
AIDWA
23 V.P. House, Rail Marg
New Delhi 110001, India

Hon. Nino Khoperia
Member of Parliament
Parliamentary Committee of Sectoral Economy
Tbilisi, Georgia

Mr. Ashok Malhotra
Programme Officer, Governance Division
United Nations Development Programme
P.O.Box No. 3059, 55, Lodi Estate
New Delhi 110003, India

Dr. Vina Mazumdar
Centre for Women's Development Studies
25 Bhai Vir Singh Marg, Gole Market
New Delhi 110001, India

WOMEN'S
POLITICAL
PARTICIPATION
AND GOOD
GOVERNANCE:
21ST CENTURY
CHALLENGES

86

Dr. Brenda Gael McSweeney
United Nations Resident Co-ordinator
    and United Nations Development
    Programme Representative
Office of the UN Resident Co-ordinator and United
    Nations Development Programme
P.O.Box No. 3059, 55 Lodhi Estate
New Delhi 110 003, India

Ms. Aparna Mehrotra
Deputy Chief Regional Programme
Regional Bureau of Latin America
    and the Caribbean
United Nations Development Programme
One United Nations Plaza
New York NY 10017, USA

Ms. Jayshree A. Mehta, Chair, GASAT
    and President,OFAN
SATWAC Foundation
A1/22 Amrapali, Sukhipura
Paldi, Ahmedabad 380007, India

Ms. Pratibha Mehta, Coordinator, LIFE programme
Management Development and Governance Division
Bureau of Development Policy
United Nations Development Programme
One United Nations Plaza
New York NY 10017, USA

Ms. Kalyani Menon-Sen, Gender Advisor
United Nations Development Programme
P.O.Box No. 3059, 55 Lodi Estate
New Delhi 110003, India

Hon. Phyllis Mitchell, Minister of State
Member of Parliament
2 National Heroes Circle, Kingston 4
Kingston, Jamaica

Ms. Enny Moaitz, Vice President
The National Council of Women
P.O. Box 1663, LAE 1663
Morobe Province, Papua New Guinea

Hon. Beth Mugo, Member of Parliament
Beth International Ltd.
Standard Building, 2nd Floor
Warabera/Standard Street, P.O. Box 42542
Nairobi, Kenya

Mrs. Usha Narayanan
First Lady of India
Rashtrapati Bhavan, New Delhi, India

Professor Sajjad Naseer
Department of Political Science
University of Punjab, Lahore, Pakistan

Ms. Aissatou Ndiongue, Deputy Mayor
Dakar, Senegal

Mr. Paul Oquist, Chief, Governance Unit
United Nations Development Programme
UN House
Saudi Pak Tower, 13th Floor
61-A, Jinnah Avenue, Blue Area, P.O. Box 1051
Islamabad, Pakistan

Mrs. Avinash Pandit, Controller, Mass Media (Retd.)
Ministry of Health & Family Welfare
Government of India
B-24, Maharani Bagh
New Delhi—110 065, India

Ms. Vibha Parathasarthy, Chairperson
National Commission for Women
2 Deen Dayal Upadhyay Marg
(Indian Council for Child Welfare Building)
New Delhi, India

Ms. Dulce Maria Pereira, President
Fundacao Cultural Palmares, Ministerio da Cultura
SBN-Q2-Ed. Central Brasilia, 1o Subsolo
Brasilia, Brasil CEP 70040-904

Mayor Sofia Prats
Municipality of Huechuraba and Member of
    the International Union of Local Authorities
    Task Force on Women
Av. Premio Nobel 5.555
Huechuraba, Chile

Dr. Sangeetha Purushothaman
1 Palmgrove Road, Victorial Layout
Bangalore 560047, India

Mayor Voahangy Razafindrakotohasina
Commune Urbaine dAntisirabe
Antsirabe 110, Madagascar

Ms. Aruna Roy
Mazdoor Kisan Shakti Sangathan
Devdungri (Kabeda), P.O. Barar
Tehsil Bhim, District Udaipur
Rajasthan 313 341, India

Ms. Sushma Swaraj
8, Tees January Marg
New Delhi—110 001, India

Prof. Zinatun Nesa Talukdar, Hon. State Minister
Ministry of Women and Children Affairs
Dhaka, Bangladesh

Ms. Teodora Tsijili-Augelaki, Vice President
Alianza de Mujeres Costarricenses
Aparatado 6851-1000
San Jose, Costa Rica

Ms. Amina Shafik Youssef
HODA
Cairo, Egypt

Dr. Poornima Vyasulu
"El Salvador"
451, 38 A Cross, 9th main, 5th Block
Jayanagar, Bangalore 560 041, India

WOMEN'S
POLITICAL
PARTICIPATION
AND GOOD
GOVERNANCE:
21ST CENTURY
CHALLENGES

88

ANNEXES

RECOMMENDATIONS OF THE BEIJING PLATFORM FOR ACTION

Strategic objective G.1. Take measures to ensure women's equal access to and full participation in power structures and decision-making

190. By Governments:

(a) Commit themselves to establishing the goal of gender balance in governmental bodies and committees, as well as in public administrative entities, and in the judiciary, including, *inter alia*, setting specific targets and implementing measures substantially increase the number of women with a view to achieving equal representation of women and men, if necessary through positive action, in all governmental and public administration positions;

(b) Take measures, including, where appropriate, in electoral systems that encourage political parties to integrate women in elective and non-elective public positions in the same proportion and at the same levels as men;

(c) Protect and promote the equal rights of women and men to engage in political activities and to freedom of association, including membership in political parties and trade unions;

(d) Review the differential impact of electoral systems on the political representation of women in elected bodies and consider, where appropriate, the adjustment or reform of those systems;

(e) Monitor and evaluate progress in the representation of women through the regular collection, analysis and dissemination of quantitative and qualitative data on women and men at all levels in various decision-making positions in the public and private sectors, and disseminate data on the number of women and men employed at various levels in Governments on a yearly basis; ensure that women and men have equal access to the full range of public appointments and set up mechanisms within governmental structures for monitoring progress in this field;

(f) Support non-governmental organizations and research institutes that conduct studies on women's participation in and impact on decision-making and the decision-making environment

(g) Encourage greater involvement of indigenous women in decision-making at all levels;

(h) Encourage and, where appropriate, ensure that government-funded organizations adopt non-discriminatory policies and practices in order to increase the number and raise the position of women in their organizations;

(i) Recognize that shared work and parental responsibilities between women and men promote women's increased participation in public life, and take appropriate measures to achieve this, including measures to reconcile family and professional life;

(j) Aim at gender balance in the lists of national candidates nominated for election or appointment to United Nations bodies, specialized agencies and other autonomous organizations of the United Nations system, particularly for posts at the senior level.

191. By political parties:

(a) Consider examining party structures and procedures to remove all barriers that directly or indirectly discriminate against the participation of women;

(b) Consider developing initiatives that allow women to participate fully in all internal policy-making structures and appointive and electoral nominating processes;

(c) Consider incorporating gender issues in their political agenda, taking measures to ensure that women can participate in the leadership of political parties on an equal basis with men.

192. By Governments, national bodies, the private sector, political parties, trade unions, employers' organizations, research and academic institutions, sub-regional and regional bodies and non-governmental and international organizations

(a) Take positive action to build a critical mass of women leaders, 0executives and managers in strategic decision-making positions;

(b) Create or strengthen, as appropriate, mechanisms to monitor women's access to senior levels of decision-making;

(c) Review the criteria for recruitment and appointment to advisory and decision-making bodies and promotion to senior positions to ensure that such criteria are relevant and do not discriminate against women;

(d) Encourage efforts by non-governmental organizations, trade union and the private sector to achieve equality between women and men in their ranks, including equal participation in their decision-making bodies and in negotiations in all areas and at all levels;

(e) Develop communications strategies to promote public debate on the new roles of men and women in society, and in the family as defined in paragraph 29 above;

(f) Restructure recruitment and career-development programmes to ensure that all women,

especially young women, have equal access to managerial, entrepreneurial, technical and leadership training, including on-the-job training;

(g) Develop career advancement programmes for women of all ages that include career planning, tracking, mentoring, coaching, training and retraining;

(h) Encourage and support the participation of women's non-governmental organizations in United Nations conferences and their preparatory processes;

(i) Aim at and support gender balance in the composition of delegations to the United Nations and other international forums.

193. By the United Nations:

(a) Implement existing and adopt new employment policies and measures in order to achieve overall gender equality, particularly at the Professional level and above, by the year 2000, with due regard to the importance of recruiting staff on as wide a geographical basis as possible, in conformity with Article 101, paragraph 3, of the Charter of the United Nations;

(b) Develop mechanisms to nominate women candidates for appointment to senior posts in the United Nations, the specialized agencies and other organizations and bodies of the United Nations system;

(c) Continue to collect and disseminate quantitative and qualitative data on women and men in decision-making and analyse their differential impact on decision-making and monitor progress towards achieving the Secretary-General's target of having women hold 50 per cent of managerial and decision-making positions by the year 2000.

194. By women's organizations, non-governmental organizations, trade unions, social partners, producers, and industrial and professional organizations:

(a) Build and strengthen solidarity among women through information, education and sensitization activities;

(b) Advocate at all levels to enable women to influence political, economic and social decisions, processes and systems, and work towards seeking accountability from elected representatives on their commitment to gender concerns;

(c) Establish, consistent with data protection legislation, databases on women and their qualification for use in appointing women to senior decision-making and advisory positions, for dissemination to Governments, regional and international organizations and private enterprise, political parties and other relevant bodies.

Strategic objective G.2. Increase women's capacity to participate in decision-making and leadership

195. By Governments, national bodies, the private sector, political parties, trade unions, employers' organizations, sub-regional and regional bodies, non-governmental and international organizations and educational institutions:

(a) Provide leadership and self-esteem training to assist women and girls, particularly those with special needs, women with disabilities and women belonging to racial and ethnic minorities to strengthen their self-esteem and to encourage them to take decision-making position;

(b) Have transparent criteria for decision-making positions and ensure that the selecting bodies have a gender-balanced composition;

(c) Create a system of mentoring for inexperienced women and, in particular, offer training, including training in leadership and decision-making, public speaking and self-assertion, as well as in political campaigning;

(d) Provide gender-sensitive training for women and men to promote non-discriminatory working relationships and respect for diversity in work and management styles;

(e) Develop mechanisms and training to encourage women to participate in the electoral process, political activities and other leadership areas.

ANNEXES

UNDP'S EXPERIENCE IN GENDER AND GOVERNANCE INSTITUTIONS

LINA HAMADEH-BANERJEE

Governance is a relatively new field for UNDP's technical co-operation activities. The conceptual framework appeared in January 1997 publication as a policy document entitled *Governance for Sustainable Human Development*. It defined *governance* as *the exercise of economic, political, and administrative authority to manage a country's affairs at all levels, comprising the mechanisms, processes and institutions through which that authority is directed. Good governance is, among other things, participatory, transparent, accountable and efficient.*

Consequently, for UNDP, governance actors go beyond the state to include the private sector and civil society. Good governance is a precondition for sustainable human development, which gives priority to the poor, generates job-led growth, advances women and protects the environment.

While UNDP's articulation of the concept of governance is relatively new, its programmatic application is not. Since the 1980s, UNDP has supported a number of initiatives for civil service reform through its Management Development Programme. These civil service reform activities were seen as catalysts in creating an enabling environment for governance activities. Then, from the outset of the 1990s, political changes world-wide led many countries to request UNDP assistance in this process.

UNDP defines government institutions as the instruments through which the state maintains its contract with its citizens. Through institutions, the state defines the rights of citizens and their responsibilities to the state and to one another. If women do not have these rights and responsibilities, they are not citizens of a state, but its subjects.

Over the years, UNDP has contributed towards enhancing women's access to government institutions and their participation in them largely through supporting women-specific programme activities. The selection criteria for all the projects listed in this annex are the following:

(a) serving as catalyst to improving women's participation in and benefit from UNDP's governance programme activities;
(b) contributing to national capacity initiatives for integrating gender concerns in governance;

WOMEN'S POLITICAL PARTICIPATION AND GOOD GOVERNANCE: 21ST CENTURY CHALLENGES

(c) providing access to networks at the local, national or international levels;

(d) innovating; and

(e) having at least a potential for replicability in other countries.

Elections

More and more, UNDP has been called upon to provide support for electoral activities, particularly in the preparation for elections. Women's participation in the election process is recognised as a critical avenue for their participation in public decision-making and political leadership; for their being perceived as a political constituency; and for their voicing their concerns so that politicians will listen.

Elections in **Bangladesh** became the basis for confrontation between the government and the opposition, leading to electoral boycotts in 1986, 1988 and in late 1990, as well as a boycott of the Parliament by the opposition in 1994. As the political environment deteriorated, the opposition demanded holding general elections under a caretaker government. This led to the creation of an Electoral Commission, a Constitutional amendment and, on 12 June 1996, a largely successful Parliamentary election under a caretaker government. UNDP provided technical support to the Government of Bangladesh, together with Canada, Denmark, Netherlands and Norway, as well as the Asia Foundation.

UNDP formulated a $10,232,600 nationally executed project for strengthening the Election Commission's capacity to plan, execute, monitor and report on elections.[99] Capacity development was directed not only to the Commission, but also to officials with election duties at the local levels, and to the electorate itself. A campaign was organised to create mass awareness for registration and consciousness of voter rights through the media, NGOs and local government officials to encourage citizens to register themselves on the electoral rolls. The project management worked with political parties to expand and develop new rules of conduct, especially with regard to the adjudication of grievances, such as the barring of women from voting. The Election Training Institute was strengthened so as to train the polling officials, the electoral inquiry committee,

party polling agents, election observer, and civic and voter education agents.

One major project activity was the organisation of a National Election Conference whose participants came not only from political parties, and the media, but NGOs and women's organisations involved in voter education.

The 1996 general election proved notable for the turnout of women voters. However, because of reports of incidents of the denial of women's right to vote, either within their homes or, more systematically, involving intimidation in the vicinity of polling booths on election day, the project aimed at reducing the obstacles facing women's full participation in elections. It did so through voter education campaigns, gender-sensitized training of election officials and the building of an electronic database of gender-disaggregated voter statistics for monitoring, analysis and reporting on voting patterns. Training materials were revised together with election manuals with special regard to their gender-sensitized content. One of the success criteria established by the project was verified high voting turnout, particularly among women.

This project, with its gender components, was an integral part of a comprehensive and integrated UNDP governance programme in Bangladesh. Complementary activities of other projects are covered in this report in different sections.

In **Zimbabwe,** the ongoing project *Women in Politics and Decision-Making*[100] stems in part from women's marginal participation in decision-making at the national and local levels remained marginal. This project approached this problem by focusing on increasing Zimbabwean women's capacity first; to participate in policy and decision-making in the various power points and second, to create a strong civil society based on rights and responsibilities. The long-term anticipated impact of this project is the foundation for an equitable distribution of power between men and women in policy formulation and implementation at the community, local and national levels.

Implemented by the Ministry of Women, has four objectives: (a) to promote a culture of recognition of women's abilities and talents; (b) to achieve

[99] Source—Project Document: Strengthening the Election Commission for Improvement in the Electoral Process *(BGD/ 96/018)*
[100] Source - Project Document: *(ZIM/96/004)* and country office reports.

WOMEN'S POLITICAL PARTICIPATION AND GOOD GOVERNANCE: 21ST CENTURY CHALLENGES

50 per cent representation of women in decision-making bodies, i.e. parliament, local councils, boards by the year 2000 (women in fact constitute 51 per cent of the country's population; (c) to equip women for participation in politics and decision-making though civic education and skills training; and (d) to identify potential women candidates for decision-making positions and bodies.

Several strategies are employed in targeting different groups, such as women who are already in decision-making in the power points; rural and urban women; and male as well as female aspirants to political power and decision-making positions. The project activities promote the full participation of women in the national, district and local elections through such activities as workshops, media campaigns, nation-wide voter education, campaigns, panel discussions, research and the production of posters, leaflets, and brochures.

One such immediate focus was the Rural District Council Elections held in 1998. Mobilisation of women was planned as supportive mechanism for assisting women to stand for office and also to mobilise the population to vote for women. The same approach was planned for the parliamentary elections of 2000. One expected outcome of the project is the examination of the quota system as a temporary measure to facilitate women's representation in all sectors.

Although **Pakistan** is one of the countries where a woman has held the office of Prime Minister, the country's political system remains male-dominated. The participation rates of Pakistani women as voters, candidates in the electoral process, and members of elected forums is minimal. The Election Commission has made several efforts to encourage more women to vote in each constituency, including the establishment of separate electoral booths for men and women and the organisation of public awareness campaigns. Nonetheless, social constraints and other institutional problems block women, minorities and other marginalised groups from full participation in the election process.

Through its 1996 Preparatory Assistance *Supporting Democratic Electoral Process in Pakistan,*[101] UNDP has assisted the Elections Commission of Pakistan and the Women's Division in developing a full-fledged project that will build the capacity of the Commission

to encourage active involvement of the general public in the governance of the country. The Preparatory assistance initiated work on creating an enabling environment for women's effective participation in politics through raising awareness of gender equity, good governance and individual responsibility at the mass levels through selected NGOs/CBOs, communities, and government agencies.

Upon project completion in July 1998, it was anticipated that a well-organised system for NGO co-ordination would be operational and that participating NGOs would better able to dialogue effectively with the government and with political party workers. It was also hoped that this assistance would augment the debate on women's role in political process in both the print and electronic media. At the same time, an increase in the number of CBOs working in their communities for women's participation in local bodies was expected to contribute to a larger number of programmes and motivational materials by NGOs on gender parity in democracy. The project is currently being evaluated.

Executive Branches

Of all three branches of government, most visible to the average citizen tends to be the Executive. Consequently, many UNDP's technical co-operation activities have supported institution-building activities within the executive branch, particularly in ministries of planning whose role had often been the inter-locutor for governments with UNDP.

Since the first World Conference on Women, held in Mexico in 1975, the United Nations has advocated the establishment of a women's advocacy unit commonly referred to as **national women's machinery** that will communicate women's needs and priorities to the government. In advocating this instrument, the United Nations has stressed that the interests of women may be best served by placing these machineries within the executive branch. Some countries have chosen to locate their national machineries in the offices of prime ministers, in a ministry such as the Ministry of Planning, or, in some cases, by the establishment of a separate ministry that focuses specifically on women's affairs.

UNDP has been providing capacity-building support to women's machineries in several countries over the last two decades. Indeed, until the 1990s, most of UNDP's assistance to the advancement of women

[101] Source—Project : PAK/96/011 from the UNDP Sub-regional Facility in Islamabad web site.

was directed to support government institutions; in that context, women's machineries tended to be seen as the most rational place for targeted women's participation in governance and politics in particular. This trend began changing as the political transformations of the 1990s created new challenges for women. Following the collapse of the Soviet Union, Eastern Europe and Central Asia, for example, underwent significant deterioration of women's access to equal opportunities. The liberalisation of markets in most of these countries promised progress, but tended to contribute to a backlash that worsened women's economic status and punished them politically. Physical violence against women also tended to increase. Some governments concerned with these regressions sought UNDP assistance for the establishment of women's machineries. Currently, projects are being implemented in **Armenia, Kyrgyzstan, Tajikistan, Turkmenistan and Turkey.**

Other projects supporting women's machineries are currently under way in areas where reconstruction and development work is intense. Following the 1994 Oslo Agreement and the establishment of the **Palestinian Authority** in the West Bank and Gaza, a mechanism for women as instituted—the Women's Affairs Council—and women's departments were created in the Ministry of Social Affairs, the Ministry of Planning and International Co-operation, the Ministry of Health and the Ministry of Youth and Sports.

UNDP provided capacity development assistance to these departments through a training project[102] that helped all four ministries in formulating and, where appropriate, implementing gender-sensitive policies and strategies. The project also provided a framework for a cross-sectoral approach to mainstreaming gender concerns into the socio-economic process. The project's conclusion anticipates that all Women's Departments would have explicitly formulated mandates, strategies, organisational charts, adequate staffing, work plans for priority activities and fund-raising schemes for the implementation of their activities and that they will have begun implementing their work plans.

As part of the preparatory work for the Fourth World Council on Women, held in Beijing in 1995,

the Government of **Lebanon**'s Reconstruction Council formed a National Commission for Lebanese Women. This later led to the establishment of the Lebanese National Women Machinery and the development of a strategy for the advancement of Lebanese women. UNDP and UNIFEM provided preparatory assistance[103] to this newly formed institution to enhance its capacity to implement the strategy and to advocate at the policy level. This assistance focused on strengthening the role of the National Commission for Lebanese Women, the NGO Committee and Women in Development units in line ministries, and the Lebanese Women's Council. It also helped the new national mechanism to develop a resource mobilisation strategy.

Legislatures

A larger number of countries are emerging as democracies. In their transitions, they need to strengthen their legislatures as to act as a check on executive privilege. UNDP has assisted a number of countries in the redevelopment of their parliaments. It has also contributed to information-sharing and networking among parliamentarians through organising regional and international meetings for them, among these one of the three forums of the 1997 International Conference on Governance for Sustainable Growth and Equity. Some of these activities have been carried out in collaboration with the International Parliamentary Union (IPU), based in Geneva.

In 1998, the Government of Belgium approved a $6 million *Programme for Strengthening Parliaments*[104] for UNDP implementation in 12 pilot countries. The programme also focuses on strengthening regional parliamentary associations and on undertaking research and analysis that contributes to the mechanisms for improving parliamentary democracy. Because of the traditional lack of representation of women in governing processes, this programme will give preference to activities targeted to redressing gender imbalances in parliamentary representation and legislative consideration. The eight-member Panel of Experts that guides programme implementation includes a specialist in gender and political participation, as well as an activist

[102] Source—Project document: Support to Established Women's Departments (PAL/96/006).
[103] Source—Project Fact Sheet: Strengthening the Lebanese national Women Machinery (LEB/97/009).
[104] Source: Programme Document: Programme of Co-operation Between The Government of Belgium and the United Nations Development Programme, December 1998.

woman parliamentarian from the Women's Caucus in Uganda.

The large integrated governance programme in **Bangladesh** had a $4 million project entitled *Strengthening Parliamentary Democracy,*[105] which has had a number of gender-significant results including the following: The 330-member Bangladeshi Parliament has reserved 30 of its seats to women candidates, who are indirectly elected by the majority party members; prior to 1997, only seven seats had been occupied by women. The Prime Minister has announced that steps will be taken to ensure direct election of women to the reserved seats and, in addition, to increase their number to 30 per cent of the total shortly after 2000, when current constitutional provisions expire. Representatives of both the Government and the Opposition have identified a number of areas in which support to the Parliament is needed to foster democratic practices: training in parliamentary practice; research support for MPs; increasing their capacity to bring gender dimensions into the policy debate, as well as into legislation; changing the Rules of Procedure to allow the Committees of the Parliament to be chaired by non-minister members of parliament to provide effective oversight; and strengthening the library facilities and the capacity of the Parliamentary Secretariat.

At its completion, this project is expected to contribute to strengthening the capacity of the Parliament not only to legislate, oversee government, and debate issues of national importance, but also to respond more effectively to the poor and to women, who constitute a majority of the poor. To enhance accountability and transparency in the parliamentary process, the project will involve civil society, media, academia, researchers and other interest groups—particularly women's groups and poverty-stricken groups—for reaching gender balance in Parliament and addressing gender issues in its deliberations. Gender training will be provided for all members of parliament. In addition, a women member of parliament caucus group was expected to begin creating linkages with the various women's organisations in the country.

In implementing the 1995 Beijing Platform for Action, **Viet Nam** adopted its own National Plan of Action for the Advancement of Vietnamese Women

by the Year 2000. Its objective was to enhance the role and position of women in leadership mechanisms and decision-making and to increase the number of women to 20 - 30 per cent of elected officials and 15–20 per cent of government and consultative bodies. In collaboration with the National Committee for the Advancement of Women and the Vietnam Women's Union, the Government of the Netherlands and UNDP funded a project[106] aiming at building national capacity for reaching the Plan's objectives by focusing on women and leadership.

This project has a multifaceted strategy: training a cadre of trainers, providing leadership training for women candidates, implementing a public information campaign and developing information resources. Local leadership training courses were provided for 144 women candidates who stood for election for the Tenth National Assembly in July 1997. These courses provided women candidates with the opportunity to deepen their understanding of the various factors influencing their political position during the election process and to assist them in identifying strategies to enhance their election prospects. Training emphasized campaigning and presentation skills and the preparation of platforms for action. Before the elections, a press conference aimed promoting a positive image of women in leadership and furthering greater representation of women in government. The proportion of women represented in the National Assembly (the highest elected decision-making body) has risen from 18 to 26 per cent, making thus putting Viet Nam the highest-ranking country in Asia and Pacific region for women in parliament.

Similar efforts were repeated for the 1999 People's Councils elections. A Manual for Women in People's Council was developed by the Viet Nam Women's Union, with the assistance from CIDA. This Manual focuses on women's leadership, the roles and functions of People's Councils, skill development and gender awareness. The focus on the latter is part of the strategy to promote an approach that will enhance gender-sensitive policies relating to working conditions and gender responsive policies and programmes. As a result, the Women's Union, together with the Youth Union and Ho Chi Minh Academy, conducted leadership training sessions in which over 1000 women have been trained.[107]

[105] Source: Project document for Strengthening Parliamentary Democracy (BGD/97/003).
[106] Source—Project document: Capacity Development for the Implementation of the National Plan of Action for the Advancement of Women (VIE/96/011).
[107] UNDP Office in Viet Nam—Case Study of UNDP Project: Leadership Training for Women- The National Assembly in Viet Nam.

UNDP'S EXPERIENCE IN GENDER AND GOVERNANCE INSTITUTIONS

With financial support from the Government of Finland, the Regional Bureau for Europe and Commonwealth of Independent States and the Gender in Development Programme in UNDP co-operated with the African European Institute in organizing an "International Conference on Gender Balance and Good Governance: African—European Dialogue on Women in Decision-Making", held in Helsinki, Finland from 25–28 September 1997.[108] The Conference was attended by participants who were largely members of the parliaments of Angola, Azerbaijan, Bosnia and Herzegovina, Botswana, Bulgaria, Burkina Faso, Burundi, Estonia, the European Parliament, Finland, Georgia, Germany, Ireland, Kyrgyzstan, Latvia, Lesotho, Lithuania, Malawi, Malta, Moldova, Mozambique, Namibia, the Netherlands, Romania, Russia, Rwanda, South Africa, Swaziland, Sweden, Switzerland, Tajikistan, Tanzania, Turkmenistan, Turkey, Ukraine, the United Kingdom, Uzbekistan, Zambia, Zimbabwe. Its agenda included a review of progress since Beijing, and national structures and institutions for gender balance, legislation for change towards gender equality, gender equality in local government strategies for economic empowerment, and the Windhoek Agenda for Gender Equality regional plan of action. This Conference provided opportunities for international and regional networking, as well as learning from the Finnish experience as an example for reaching the dual goals of gender balance and good governance.

Judicial Support

Nowhere do women fare worse than with gender-biased law and its agents, from police officers through Ministers of Justice.

UNDP has been instrumental in following up on the ratification and implementation of the CEDAW in ten Pacific Island Countries.[109] A Regional Consultation held in Nadi, 20-24 July 1998 and attended by 50 participants resulted in an agreement among the Secretariat of the Pacific Community, ESCAP and UNDP to provide continued support to post-Beijing initiatives through targeted technical assistance to promote community awareness, institutional strengthening and capacity-building

of mechanisms for the advancement of women in the Pacific Region. The participants prepared a matrix of strategic actions for a region-wide programme to this end.

In **Sri Lanka,** UNDP, UNIFEM and UNFPA have provided assistance to the Ministry of Women's Affairs[110] aiming at strengthening the capacities of the Ministry, the Women's Bureau, the National Committee on Women, the Department of National Planning, relevant ministries, Provincial/District Secretariats, and NGOs in a variety of areas, including the promotion of legal literacy and gender-sensitization of the police force and members of the judiciary. These efforts are linked to another UNDP-funded project aimed at enhancing the intellectual and institutional capacity of the Legal Draftsman's Department at both the national and provincial level, including computerizing the drafting process and consolidating all national and provincial laws, amendments and subsidiary legislation. Through activities carried out in conjunction with the Sri Lanka Institute for Development Administration (SLIDA), new law syllabi and teaching materials are also being introduced to make legislation more compatible with CEDAW and to enhance the Convention's implementation.[112]

In **Kenya** UNDP launched two projects[113] in 1998 valued at $1.37 million to strengthen the legal and political status of women and to increase their participation in government and in conflict resolution processes. The initiatives were to help prepare and disseminate public awareness materials on women's rights, and to conduct training programmes. Key institutions including the Attorney General's Office, the National Assembly and the Judiciary and Electoral Commission were also supported by these projects, which were being executed by two international NGOs: the League of Women Voters and the International Federation of Women Lawyers.

During the 1990s, a number of **Latin American** countries embarked on judicial reform, requesting UNDP assistance to enhance the administration of justice through improvement of structure and administration of the court system, and training of legal personnel ranging from judges to lawyers and

WOMEN'S POLITICAL PARTICIPATION AND GOOD GOVERNANCE: 21ST CENTURY CHALLENGES

[108] Source—Jeff Balch and Nola Caffey, editors, 1998. International Conference on Gender Balance and Good Governance: African—European Dialogue on Women in Decision-Making: Conference Report: the African European Institute, Amsterdam, the Netherlands.
[109] Source: Support to CEDAW Activities in the Pacific - PMI/97/004.
[110] Source—project document: Enhancing the Capability of the Ministry of Women's Affairs for Mainstreaming Gender in Development (SRL/97/206).
[111] Project document: Enhancing Infrastructure for Legal Draftsman's Department (SRL/97/297).
[112] Response to the MDGD Human Rights Questionnaire received from the UNDP office in Sri Lanka.
[113] UNDP Flash.

court staff. While support to reform activities such as that in Nicaragua, did not specifically target women's concerns, in most cases the beneficiaries of an improved judicial system have been the poor and minorities, where barriers against women have been most pronounced.

Human Rights

Early in 1998 and after several consultations within UNDP and with external partners, UNDP adopted its policy document on *Integrating Human Rights with Sustainable Development*, in which gender equality and poverty reduction programmes are seen as providing enabling mechanisms for empowering people to claim their human rights.

The policy document strengthens a variety of continuing UNDP efforts. These include work on refugees and their resettlement and integration, notably in Cambodia. It encompasses a specific gender programme in Pakistan that stresses women's strategic needs, including their right to mobility, a prime requirement of full participation in development; practical efforts to this end include the Ministry of Transport, private transportation enterprises, and traffic police. It extends, too, to the symposium on female genital mutilation convened in Nairobi, Kenya by UNDP[114] and UNICEF June 1998 brought together policy makers, doctors, media representatives and NGOs to identify ways to prevent this harmful, controversial practice. They jointly examined the psychological trauma it produces; the need for greater advocacy, education, policy guidelines and health awareness; human and legal rights; and religious issues arising from principles of Christianity and Islam. A plan of action identifying specific measures to stop female genital mutilation was proposed. In addition, UNDP has supported related advocacy and public awareness activities in Kenya.

In commemorating the 50th Anniversary of the Declaration on Human Rights, UNDP, together with 11 other United Nations organisations joined forces in planning a **campaign to combat violence against women in Africa.** Coordinated by UNIFEM, this campaign sought to increase public awareness on domestic violence, violence against women during war and civil strife, female genital mutilation and the importance of women's political participation in reconstruction as well as normal development efforts.

Chapter 8 of the present collection details a comparable campaign in 20 countries of Latin America and the Caribbean. Moreover, this **Inter-Agency Campaign on Violence Against Women and Girls in Latin America and the Caribbean** was among the first projects funded by the United Nations Foundation, an organisation founded by Ted Turner to serve United Nations causes.

Conclusion

This annex attempted to synthesize a sample of UNDP projects (mostly women specific) that were under the category of support to governing institutions; these largely comprise the mechanisms, processes and institutions through which citizens and groups articulate their interests, exercise their legal rights, meet their obligations and mediate their differences. As demonstrated in the different chapters of this volume, women's roles in decision-making have not reached their potential, largely due to lack of recognition of the unequal opportunities between men and women. Women remain excluded from all aspects of governance that affect their lives and their full participation and benefit from development on equal footing to men. It is because of this that UNDP has attempted to contribute to assist women to catch up with this backlog of inequality that leads to their exclusion.

---

[114] Source—UNDP's electronic periodical *Flash*.